MANY THOUGH[T]

Christian passages for meditation and secondary school worship

Compiled by
JAN THOMPSON

Hodder & Stoughton
LONDON   SYDNEY   AUCKLAND   TORONTO

I dedicate this book and its author's royalties to **Christian Aid**, an ecumenical Church charity which works for justice and the relief of human suffering in the Third World. It aims to restore human dignity by helping people to help themselves.

> Give us, dear Lord, a vision of our world as your love would make it:
> – a world where the weak are protected,
>   and none go hungry or poor;
> – a world where benefits are shared,
>   so that everyone can enjoy them;
> – a world where different peoples and cultures
>   live with tolerance and mutual respect;
> – a world where peace is built with justice,
>   and justice is fired by love.
> And give us the courage to build it.

(Brian Wren, for Christian Aid)

British Library Cataloguing in Publication Data
Many thoughts.
   1. Christian Life – *Devotional works*
   I. Thompson, Jan
   242

ISBN 0-340-54438-4

First published 1991

© 1991 Jan Thompson

All rights reserved. No part of this publication may be reproduced or transmitted in any form or by any means, electronic or mechanical, including photocopy, recording, or any information storage and retrieval system, without permission in writing from the publisher or under licence from the Copyright Licensing Agency Limited. Further details of such licences (for reprographic reproduction) may be obtained from the Copyright Licensing Agency Limited, of 33–34 Alfred Place, London WC1E 7DP.

Typeset by Litho Link Ltd, Welshpool, Powys, Wales
Printed in Great Britain for the educational publishing division of Hodder and Stoughton Ltd, Mill Road, Dunton Green, Sevenoaks, Kent by Athenaeum Press Ltd, Newcastle upon Tyne.

Contents

Preface

Human Nature
Self knowledge   1
Which is my real self?   2, 3
The inner person affects our outward actions   4
To some extent we make our own futures   5
The human ideal   6
Can we make sense of life?   7, 8
How small we are!   9
We must trust that there is meaning in life   10
We are physical, mental and spiritual beings   11, 12
A crisis or tragedy may help us discover our true identity   13, 14
We must first accept ourselves   15–18
Being honest with ourselves   19, 20
A worthwhile life takes effort   21, 22
Courage to live out our destiny.   23, 24
Something more to life   25
Love gives life meaning   26, 27
Materialism can never really satisfy us   28, 29
What are true riches?   30
Alienation and inner renewal   31
Finding the true self   32

The religious quest
The importance of knowing God   33
Life has meaning   34
Keeping a space for God   35, 36
Are we alone?   37–41
It takes faith   42, 43
We 'walk in two worlds' – the material and the spiritual   44–46
Religion and art   47, 48
The need for religion   49, 50
Religion is not an easy option, but a quest for truth   51–54
Religion and science   55–58
Human nature is religious   59, 60
Don't give up your search for God   61
Belief and doubt   62–65
Whom can we trust in times of need?   66, 67
God is to be found at the heart of everyday life   68–72
God is made visible in loving actions   73
The voice of God speaks in creation   74–77
Coming to know God   78

'Dwell secretly in the presence of God'   79
God's 'still, small voice'   80
Conversion experiences   81, 82
The Power of the Bible to convert   83
'The quiet assurance of an inner voice'   84

God
Believing   85, 86
Making God in our image   87, 88
Can we prove God?   89
The limitations of God-talk   90
Evidence of God   91, 92
God or Materialism?   93, 94
Evolution witnesses to the existence of God   95, 96
God is Creator   97, 98
God is just   99
God is eternal   100
God is Love   101–105
God the Trinity   106
God the Holy Spirit   107–109
God the Father   110
God the Son   111–114
The love of God in Jesus Christ   115–117
Jesus was true to himself   118–120

Loving others
1 Corinthians 13   121–123
'The love of God operating in the human heart'   124–127
Giving and getting   128
'When I was hungry ...'   129
Made in the image of God   130, 131
Not imposing our own solutions   132
Each of us is a person   133
Friendship   134, 135
The Christian ideal of friendship   136, 137
We are 'people who need people'   138, 139
Getting and having are no substitutes for being loved   140–143
The love of God in action   144
The Beatitudes   145

Prayer
(A number of points about prayer)   146, 147
The human need for prayer   148, 149
No longer alone   150–152

Prayer helps us to focus our minds on God 153–155
Asking-prayers 156
Prayer moves us beyond the superficialities of life 157, 158
'When I try to pray deliberately, it is gone' 159, 160
Prayer in everyday life 161, 162
Prayer as a way of life 163–165
Contemplation 166–168
William Barclay on prayer 169
Prayer is . . . 170, 171

Peace
Peace begins with me 172, 173
Help us to see the best in people 174, 175
Trying to love our enemies 176–178
Forgiveness 179–185
Christ's arms outstretched in peace 186

Suffering
'Faith in the City' 187
Why is there suffering? 188
Does God send suffering? 189, 190
Suffering is not an 'act of God' 191
Does God stop suffering? 192
Let's stop asking 'Why?' 193, 194
Hopelessness 195
Hopefulness 196, 197
We can learn from our suffering 198–201
The comfort of God 202
Those in need can enrich us 203, 204
The grit and the pearl 205
Wanted – just as he was 206
'The presence of God in the heart of the dark' 207, 208

Death
Death is a fact of life 209, 210
Facing up to death 211–215
Live for today 216
Our attitude to death affects our attitude to life 217, 218
An out-of-the-body experience 219
A plea for more openness about death and bereavement 220
Separation from loved ones 221–223
Approaching death 224–226
Belief in life after death 227–231

Index of Authors

Acknowledgements

The Publishers would like to thank the following for permission to reproduce material in this volume:

A M Heath for extract 59.

Aitken & Stone Ltd for extract 160.

Anthony Sheil Associates Ltd for extracts 156, 159 177.

Cassell (Mowbray) for extracts 1, 64, 78, 89, 90, 95, 96, 99, 100, 104, 114, 120, 121, 129, 135, 147, 169, 173, 188, 189, 191, 213, 218, 223, 228.

Church Times for extract 106.

Collins for extracts 3, 13, 15, 16, 21, 23, 26, 27, 35, 37, 38, 41, 58, 66, 70, 71, 73, 78, 84, 87, 105, 123, 124, 139, 165, 167, 172, 175, 176, 179, 184, 208, 212, 229.

Coventry Cathedral for extract 183.

Darton Longman & Todd Ltd for extracts 2, 11, 36, 72, 79, 103, 112, 113, 115, 116, 126, 130, 140, 150, 151, 158, 166, 181, 192, 195, 199, 227.

Firethorn Press (imprint of Waterstone & Co Ltd) for extracts 18, 55, 226.

Hodder & Stoughton for extracts 17, 31, 33, 43, 44, 45, 57, 67, 81, 91, 141, 148, 157, 161, 190, 193, 196, 197, 200, 201, 204, 207, 211, 216, 217, 225, 230.

International Thomson Publishing Services Ltd for extract 53.

Lutterworth Press for extracts 74, 76, 122, 163, 117, 118, 162.

Mrs Louise Stephenson for extracts 8, 210

New Internationalist for extracts 49, 50, 51, 60.

Penguin Books Ltd for extracts 25, 160.

Quaker Home Service for extract 80.

Robson Books Ltd for extracts 20, 42.

SCM Press Ltd for extracts 4, 9, 12, 24, 32, 83, 86, 93, 94, 98, 107, 136, 137, 149, 155, 224.

Southwark Diocesan Office for extract 69.

SPCK for extracts 153, 168, 164, 219.

Unwin Hyman Ltd for extract 42.

Every effort has been made to trace and acknowledge ownership of copyright. The publishers will be glad to make suitable arrangements with any copyright holders whom it has not been possible to contact.

Preface

Many Thoughts contains well over two hundred extracts, most of which have not appeared in anthologies before. The passages come from Christian sources, but the thoughts they contain about human life and relationships, suffering and death, and the religious quest, are relevant to anyone who is prepared to think deeply about life. They are therefore suitable as Christian meditations, as well as readings for secondary school worship 'of a broadly Christian character', particularly for older students.

It is hoped that this resource will set off trains of thought in the minds of those who read them, perhaps sparked off by just one sentence or phrase from each passage. For those preparing secondary school worship, these readings can be used as they stand or put into your own words, abbreviated or added to. The busy teacher will find many people's thoughts on the spiritual dimension of life collected here under eight broad headings.

HUMAN NATURE

Self knowledge

1. Juvenal, the Roman satirist, wrote: 'The maxim "Know thyself" comes down to us from the skies; it should be imprinted in the heart, and stored in the memory . . . Cicero said that, since the saying was greater than the human mind could have envisaged, it was attributed to God. Maybe Thomas Carlyle was wise when he spoke of, 'the folly of that impossible precept "Know thyself", till it be translated into the partially possible one, "Know what thou canst work at".' If a man cannot know himself, he can at least know what he can and cannot do.

(Testament of Faith W. Barclay, p. 19)

Which is my real self?

2. Throughout the day we are a succession of social personalities, sometimes unrecognisable to others or even to ourselves . . . From time to time something authentic shows through, when we forget ourselves our deep reality may take over, in moments when we are carried away by joy so that we forget who might be looking at us, forget to stand aside and look at ourselves, or when we are unselfconscious in moments of extreme pain, moments when we have a deep sense of sadness or of wonder. At these moments we see something of the true person that we are. But no sooner have we seen, than we often turn away because we do not want to confront this person face to face. We are afraid of him, he puts us off.

Nevertheless this is the only real person there is in us. And God can save this person, however repellent he may be, because it is a true person. God cannot save the imaginary person that we try to present to him, or to others or ourselves.

(Courage to Pray, A. Bloom, pp. 18–19)

Dietrich Bonhoeffer is famous as a German pastor and theologian who was executed in 1945 for plotting against Hitler. While in prison, he wrote this poem. It contrasts the outward impression we may make on others with our own inner fears and feelings. It prompts us to ask 'Who am I?

3 Who am I? They often tell me
I stepped from my cell's confinement
Calmly, cheerfully, firmly,
Like a squire from his country-house.
Who am I? They often tell me
I used to speak to my warders
Freely and friendly and clearly,
As though it were mine to command.
Who am I? They also tell me
I bore the days of misfortune
Equably, smilingly, proudly,
Like one accustomed to win.

Am I then really all that which other men tell of?
Or am I only what I myself know of myself?
Restless and longing and sick, like a bird in a cage,
Struggling for breath, as though hands were
   compressing my throat,
Yearning for colours, for flowers, for the voices of birds,
Thirsting for words of kindness, for neighbourliness,
Tossing in expectation of great events,
Powerlessly trembling for friends at an infinite distance,
Weary and empty at praying, at thinking, at making,
Faint, and ready to say farewell to it all?

Who am I? This or the other?
Am I one person to-day and to-morrow another?
Am I both at once? A hypocrite before others.
And before myself a contemptibly woebegone weakling?
Or is something within me still like a beaten army,
Fleeing in disorder from victory already achieved?

Who am I? They mock me, these lonely questions of mine.
Whoever I am, Thou knowest, O God, I am thine!

(*Letters and Papers from Prison*, D. Bonhoeffer, p. 173)

The inner person affects our outward actions

4   Each of us is continually at work creating his own biography or life story. Those who chronicle the events of life in biography or autobigraphy usually list the important deeds that involve time and place, actions and reactions. These are the objective facts of life. But behind the things that are worked out in space and time is another important world, one that is not as easily available to the biographer, but which is probably more important. This is the realm of thought and feeling, the inner world of being where the decisions are made that reveal themselves in external events . . .

Behind the things we do there is always the person we are. The realm of inner meanings and personal values is the seedbed in which we germinate the motives and actions that become the objective record of our living, our personal life story.

(*Understanding Prayer*, E. Jackson p. 161)

To some extent we make our own futures

5   The most serious aspect of delusions is that they tend to be habit forming, and the habits formed in youth can become tyrants in old age. I recall one night while I was in the seminary, waiting in the corridor of our infirmary while the Brother Infirmarian was tucking two bed-ridden priests in for the night. One of them was bitter and complaining, completely ungrateful. The other thanked the Brother and told him he would say an extra prayer for him before falling asleep. A sudden intuition gripped and frightened me. One day I would be one of those two priests: selfish and cantankerous or loving and grateful. But I knew, as I stood in the corridor of the infirmary, that the decision would not be made in the twilight of my life. It would be made in the young, formative years. It was being made then. Our yesterdays lie heavily upon our todays, and our todays lie heavily upon our tomorrows.

(*He touched Me*, J. Powell, pp. 29–30)

The human ideal

6 God, help me to be truly human,
Help me to be able to appreciate
and bring out the best in everyone around me.
Help me to be able to give of the best in myself.
   Many people think that to be human is
to make mistakes, to hate, to be imperfect.
But this is not true.
When Jesus was on earth,
he showed us the way
in which we should live.
   Man is not like the animal.
He does not exist, he lives.
He does not feed, he eats.
He does not mate, he loves.
He does not breed, he co-creates.
   You have created man,
so that he is capable
to appreciate consciously
all the gifts
that you have given him.
Lord, help me to appreciate all
that you have given me.
Help me to be truly human.

(*The One who Listens*, Hollings and Gullick, p. 35–6)

Can we make sense of Life?

7 I wonder why people are here on the Earth
I wonder why there is death and birth
I wonder what is the point of living
Why are we talking? and why are we giving?

These ultimate questions have puzzled Man
Why the world's here, why it began?
Why are there wars and why do we fight?
Why are things wrong? and why are things right?

These ultimate questions have puzzled us so
What are the answers, does anyone know?
Why is there living and why is there dying?
Why are some people laughing and some people crying?

Why are some countries rich and some countries poor?
What is this thing 'LIFE' and what's it all for?
Is there a heaven up in the sky?
And where do we all go when we die?

('I Wonder', Paula Bishop (13), *It's Important to Me*)

8 What is this existence which we call life? What is the self awareness which we call consciousness? Does the fact that we exist mean anything? Philosophers, poets and probably every human being who has ever lived has at some time asked themselves what is the meaning of life: why are we here? It isn't easy to begin to think about, and there may not be a simple, straightforward answer. Certainly no-one can answer the riddle for us. It is up to each of us to work out our own answer. It may be helpful to think in terms of what gives our *own* lives meaning – what makes *us* feel that living is worthwhile? Is it the love of our family and friends? Our pleasure and enjoyments of various kinds? And what can *we* contribute to the meaning of our life, and to the meaning of the lives of others? It may be that the meaning of life *for us* is related to the meaning of life for humankind generally.

(L. Stephenson)

How small we are!

9 Last evening I sat for a long while on the brow of a Vermont hill ... The wind whispered gently in a grove of pines behind me. A full moon rising in the east dimly outlined the White Mountains. A solitary light in a farmhouse in the valley below showed that its tenant was still about. The bark of a dog resounded from another direction and penetrated the silence of the night with friendliness. Overhead the Milky Way stretched itself from the northern horizon to the south as far as the eye could see. We are a part of that galaxy and yet it seemed separated and far off. A jet bomber from the nearby airbase streaked across the sky, adding its running lights to the Milky Way and seeming more nearly a part of it than I did in my thoughtful observance. The light in the valley went out, leaving only the moon to flood the landscape with its light. I realized once again how feeble man's incandescent lamps are compared with the moon. The bomber with its pinpoint of light dotting the sky streamed out of sight, leaving the Milky Way uncluttered by man as it had been for untold billions of years. In solitude I pondered how little man and his knowledge, his science, his efforts at control really touch the infinite and timeless works of God. We delude only ourselves if we think we are the masters of creation. We find ourselves only when we have the courage to face the reality of a creation that reaches out endlessly in space and time in all directions.

(*Understanding Prayer*, E. Jackson, pp. 15–16)

We must trust that there is meaning in life

10 Man can bear great physical hardship, but what he cannot bear is the sense of meaninglessness. We must find some way in which our lives count, in which they seem important, or we go mad. The ultimate enemy is not pain or disease or physical hardship, evil as these may be, but triviality. What is terrible for men and women is the conviction that they are not needed, that they contribute nothing, and that their lives add up to no enduring meaning.

(*Travelling Light*, E. Trueblood, p. 61)

We are physical, mental and spiritual beings

11 Living spiritually is more than living physically, intellectually or emotionally. It embraces all that: but it is larger, deeper and wider. It concerns the core of your humanity. It's possible to lead a very wholesome, emotionally rich and 'sensible' life without being a spiritual person: that is, without knowledge or personal experience of the terrain where the meaning and goal of our human existence are hidden.

The spiritual life has to do with the heart of existence. I find the word 'heart' a good word. I don't mean by it the seat of our feelings as opposed to the seat of our thoughts. By 'heart' I mean the centre of our being, the 'place' where we are most ourselves, where we are most human, where we are most real. In that sense the heart is the focus of the spiritual life.

(Letters of Marc, H. Nouwen, pp. 3–4)

12 Creative wholeness cannot be achieved without spiritual growth . . . Physical growth depends on the glands and proper nutrition. Mental growth comes through education and experience. Spiritual growth, however, is a personal responsibility and a personal achievement.

It is distressing to see a mentally and physically well-developed person whose spiritual growth is stunted. Yet, without the discipline of a prayerful approach to life many persons exist at a level hardly beyond that of highly endowed animals. Spiritual growth, while not a lost art, has been sadly neglected in our culture.

Spiritual growth starts with desire. More often than not the desire is arrived at negatively. Persons back into spiritual interests because they have found their lives meaningless, a desert place devoid of beauty and purpose.

(Understanding Prayer, E. Jackson, p. 45)

A crisis or a tragedy, which strips us of our illusions, may help us to discover our true identity

13 The realisation of your true identity consists primarily in detaching yourself from those attributes that are superficial but which you, in your blind ignorance, consider essential to your being. In other words, the movement towards the real is first and foremost a progressive stripping from yourself of illusions. This stripping is never really voluntary. It comes to us through those events we call tragedies, or, at the very least, disappointments. We would not seek the real, the unchangeable, the reliable if we could live happily in the world of illusion with all its glamour and false security. But the course of life is punctuated by episodes, not infrequently of long duration, in which those things we have held dear are taken from us. It may be the wealth of a rich man, or the life of one who is dear to us, or our health, or even our reputation. It may be the work that sustained us, or even a special gift on which we relied . . .

It is no use telling someone who is in severe distress that it is all useful experience for the growth of his own soul . . . Yet such a person may be nearer the great discovery of his own true being than one who is shielded against adversity by pleasant outer circumstances.

(*Summons to Life*, M. Israel, p. 18)

14 The problem is that the starting-point for the search is often a dim awareness of the unhealed or wounded parts of the personality. When confronted by pain we react in the same way as we do to anxiety; we can either try to go back, or freeze where we are, or have the courage to struggle through the darkness . . . People at the crossroads of life, when confronted by crisis or tragedy or simply by a dim, unexpressed need, can either pass the buck by blaming others, or their stars or fate or God . . . or they can take the risk of change and of finding their own creative personal solution.

(*God for Nothing*, R. MacKenna, pp. 119, 120)

We must first accept ourselves, and learn to love ourselves, if we are to do anything meaningful with our lives

15 In the beginning, all creation was loved into being. He made rare and hidden things full of light and beauty. He smiled through the mystery, and even the darkness was filled with his sweetness.

Then, with great joy, his love conceived its most beautiful miracle of all, his most treasured creation, and so from the dawn of time he carried you in his heart until now. Nothing in creation is more beautiful or more loved than you – nothing could ever take your place in his heart.

Within you lies the purest power of all, the seed of tenderness and love. If for a single moment we saw how intimately we are cherished and held in his arms, fear would be banished for ever and our faces would reflect his warmth and his joy always.

(*All Shall Be Well*, M. Meegan. p. 17)

16 To love yourself is to accept yourself as you are, and to thank God that you are as He made you . . . It means an open-hearted acceptance of our whole nature, the good and the bad, the radiant and the dark, without judgement, and a dedication of one's whole being, weak and defective though it may be, to God's service . . .

The constructive use of a defect leads to greater compassion, firstly toward other people with similar impediments and finally towards ourselves. . .

We can do nothing if we hate ourselves, or feel that all our actions are doomed to failure because of our own worthlessness. We have to take ourselves, good and bad alike, on trust before we can do anything.

(*Summons to Life*, M. Israel, pp. 66–67)

17 God, help me to stop making comparisons.

Let me remember that each life must follow its own course, and that what happens to other people has absolutely nothing to do with what happens to me.

Help me to stop trying to judge – either others, society, or you. Help me to judge only my own performance in the light of the talent, health, and opportunities you have given me.

When I fail, help me to stop blaming other people for my failures, God – or blaming you.

But help me not to blame myself too much either.

Help me to keep faith in myself, as well as faith in your will for me.

(*I've Got to Talk to Somebody, God*, M. Holmes, p. 74–75)

18 It is not what we know but what we are willing to learn that is important! And we must begin with self-realization, for the whole universe resides within each one of us individually, and the sun was made to rise and set for a single soul: yours! . . .

As you prepare to embark on your next step of personal endeavor you need only seek the answers to the questions 'Who am I' and 'Why am I here'? and when you arrive at that point where you would not change places with any other living soul, you have begun your journey in earnest . . .

Enter with *Courage* and never separate strength from compassion.
Enter with *Wisdom* and never separate justice from charity.
Enter with *Joy* and never separate love from labour.
Enter with *Faith* and never separate fact from imagination.
Enter with *Passion* and never separate desire from responsibility.
Enter with *Dignity* and never separate folly from human behaviour.
Enter with *Pride* and never separate humility from achievement.
Enter with *Prudence* and never separate generosity from thrift.
Enter with *Curiosity* and never separate inspiration from potential.
Enter with *Serenity* and never separate laughter from grief.
Enter with *Love* and never separate spirit from flesh.

(by M. Sheen, in *What I Believe*, ed. M. Booth, pp. 100, 101, 102)

Being honest with ourselves

19 Perhaps the biggest thing of all is telling the truth to ourselves. I think you know what I mean. You must have noticed how easily we can defend our meanest actions not to others but to ourselves. We can excuse our bad temper – 'after all he deserved it'; our dishonesty – 'after all they won't miss the money'; our spite, our slander. That is the most dangerous form of untruth, building a dream-picture of ourselves completely remote from the facts, a false picture, shatteringly untrue.

(Last Thing at Night, H. Lavery, p. 17)

20 Lord, you have a minute?
This is about sulking. People sulking.
Well, to be honest, Lord, not people; me.
I sulk, Lord.
I go silent and black-thoughted;
Become glowering and covered in frowns and lines.
And nobody suffers but me.

Teach me to laugh it off, Lord.
It's important, honest.
Teach me to get over it faster,
To be normal (whatever *that* is)
   and have a sense of proportion.
Not a lot to ask, Lord.
Sulking is living in a dark room,
   in the wrong spectacles, in a draught.
And if people are nice to you, Lord,
   and 'cope' with you,
You feel ten times worse.

Sulking magnifies its own cause, Lord.
Is a fairground mirror looked into
   with eyes of distorted gaze.
You can't win, it's ridiculous.
Help me win, Lord, help me not be ridiculous.

('Old Sulky' in *You have a minute, Lord?* D. Kossoff, p. 51)

A worthwhile life takes effort

21 It is easy to fool ourselves that on the surface we are doing the best we can, we are OK, but the more we question and examine our lives the more we realize that we could become better. If we stop growing we start dying; we are alive only in as far as we are receptive and alert and ready to make changes in an open and frank way. If we begin to see the beauty inside us and the power of love ready to come out, we will be willing to change some of the defences and walls that we have built, to open up that love and offer it in frail and uncertain hands to those around us.

(*All Shall Be Well*, M. Meegan, pp. 76–77)

22 We know that nothing worthwhile is ever achieved easily.
The enjoyment of playing a musical instrument
does not come without hours of practice;
Being able to speak in a foreign language
means learning the vocabulary;
Sports become more enjoyable
the more competent we become at them:
The exhilaration of a fast ski run,
only comes after many falls on the nursery slopes.
Achievements in all walks of life –
in work, in hobbies, and in relationships –
come with time and effort.
LORD, help us to be ready to make sacrifices,
So that we may lead worthwhile lives.

Amen

(J. Thompson)

Courage to live out our destiny

23   We are social animals. We care very much what people think of us and what they say. All too often we prefer to be cautious rather than open about how we feel. It is easier to keep our feelings to ourselves than risk them being laughed at or rejected. There are many people ready to take you down a peg or two, or to deflate your ego. Whatever you do, there will always be someone to volunteer a criticism.

Everyone from St Francis and Gandhi to Martin Luther King is a victim of jealousies, judgements, even persecutions. All goodness exposes itself to being attacked. Little children are told to be quiet and not to ask so many questions. Young people are told they cannot change the world and to grow up and to be realistic, to stop dreaming, walk the middle path and have some sense. We are told to stick within our limits. All the time we are offered advice. When we are old we are told we are past it, to take it easy. But when Christ came, he said, 'Yes, you can change the world. It is OK to dream and live your inner hope into reality . . .'

People will always pull you down and have a go at you. So what? You are bigger and greater than the mud thrown your way. Live what is inside and don't be afraid. That is the call of Christ, to live what is within your heart.

(*All Shall Be Well*, M. Meegan, pp. 61–62)

24   A wealthy, highly respected man, when being congratulated on his eightieth birthday, said, 'Many persons think I have had a good life. I have done some good things and I have accumulated lots of money. But I know I won't live much longer. I have invested my life energies in the things I must leave behind. In all honesty I must admit my life is a failure. When I was young I wanted to be a missionary, but I lacked courage. Nothing else has ever satisfied me.' When one denies the major commitment of life, no substitute is ever quite good enough. Some deep inner standard keeps passing its self-judgement, and no one can ever get away from himself. True joy is to be found only when the best self finds its way to fulfillment. Nothing less is able to satisfy the depths of being.

(*Understanding Prayer*, E. Jackson, p. 84)

Something more to life

25 My dear Alice,

It was good to get your letter ...

The last time I saw you, you were two, blonde and cherubic. Now, I gather, you are eighteen, you dye your hair black and green with vegetable dye, and your mother, my sister, is perturbed ... I shall not interfere between the two of you: I shall confine myself to the matters you raise.

Namely, Jane Austen and her books. You tell me, in passing, that you are doing a college course in English Literature, and are obliged to read Jane Austen; that you find her boring, petty and irrelevant and, that as the world is in crisis, and the future catastrophic, you cannot imagine what purpose there can be in your reading her.

My dear child! My dear pretty little Alice, now with black and green hair.

How can I hope to explain Literature to you, with its capital 'L'? You are bright enough. You could read when you were four. But then, sensibly, you turned to television for your window on the world: you slaked your appetite for information, for stories, for beginnings, middles and ends, with the easy tasty substances of the screen in the living room, and ... no doubt in your bedroom too. You lulled yourself to sleep with visions of violence, and the cruder strokes of human action and reaction; stories in which every simple action has a simple motive, nothing is inexplicable, and even God moves in an un-mysterious way.

And now you realize this is not enough: you have an inkling there is something more, that your own feelings and responses are a thousand times more complex than this tinny televisual representation of reality has ever suggested: you have, I suspect and hope, intimations of infinity, of the romance of creation, of the wonder of love, of the glory of existence; you look around for companions in your wild new comprehension, your sudden vision, and you see the same zonked-out stares, the same pale faces and dyed cotton-wool hair, and you turn, at last, to education, to literature, and books — and find them closed to you.

(*Letters to Alice*, F. Weldon, pp. 11, 12)

Love gives life meaning

26 What is the most important thing we have to achieve while on earth? Is it material gain – which we have to relinquish and pass on to others? Is it power and prestige – which drop from us as soon as we lose authority over others? Is it intellectual knowledge – which is superseded by new developments almost before the world has had time to assess its own contribution? Is it physical pleasure – with the body ageing from its very moment of birth?

No, none of these can be the great work of man, though each is important in its own right in helping to integrate the personality within the wider context of the world. But as an end in itself, neither gain, nor power, nor knowledge, nor pleasure, can suffice, because all of these are submerged in the finality of bodily death. There is only one thing that can survive personal death, and that is love. For in love we are no longer circumscribed, finite units, but are members one of another.

(*Summons to Life*, M. Israel, pp. 137–138)

27 We need to give of ourselves if we are to become the full potential that God in his extraordinary and irrational generosity wanted us to be. Inside us there is a miracle. If you have ever seen the ocean and how vast it is, . . . or looked up and seen the galaxy, which to our minds is almost infinite, close your eyes and remember that the power of love that exists inside you is even greater than all of the universe. It is deeper and wider than the created world and expands into eternity . . . The essential sadness of humanity is that many of us live without realizing the promise and gift of God, and as his children we will inherit the deepest and fullest joy of all, which is to love each other and the source of love for ever.

If we do not see inside ourselves the gift of life and the promise of being loved always, life turns into a rather urbane existence full of trivia and pettiness; it remains unsanctified by the fullness of God.

(*All Shall Be Well*, M. Meegan, p. 37)

Materialism can never really satisfy us

28 Barns are never big enough. Imagination can always erect greater ones and it is in the field of disordered imagination that anxiety breeds and festers. The contemporary disease is imaginary poverty; it is no less disabling than imaginary illness. Most people in the West have sufficient but do not enjoy their sufficiency; plenty does not bring peace, but, like an addictive drug instils a desire for more and more, is by definition, comparative, not complete. So there is frenzy, scramble, strikes and rumours of strikes. These are the sorry symptoms of a society not poor but sick, not deprived but discontented.

(Reflections, H. Lavery, p. 48)

29 Happiness becomes equated with 'having' and taking things for one's very own. Of course man needs to 'have' a certain number of things, a certain standard of living, before he can start to realise his potential, but the other side of the coin is the danger that he will only understand his potential in terms of how much he can 'have'. Surrounded as we are by belongings, it is as if we cease to 'have' them, and they start to 'have' us; they become all-important to us, we define ourselves in terms of them, and in the end they swallow us up . . .

The effect of this is to alienate us from our fellow man because he is a potential rival, and from the world itself because we no longer see ourselves as part of it or respect its rights in itself . . . instead we see the world as an 'it', a thing, an object to gratify our desires.

Finally we are alienated from our very selves because we have surrendered our freedom of being to a compulsion.

(God for Nothing, R. MacKenna, pp. 24–25*)*

What are true riches?

30   Lord, it's hard to get the balance right.
When someone mentions riches,
my mind walks to the bank.
I measure it in things.
In walletfuls, in bricks and mortar.
Things you never had,
and didn't even want.
Because you knew they didn't last.

But, Lord, I'm anchored to them.
Stuck, limpet-fast, to earth,
and sometimes it seems
not all your love
can prise me loose.

And yet I know the truth.
The richness that you offer
far transcends the things I hold so tight.
And finds fulfilment,
not in holding on,
but giving up.

I know.
The trouble is
the seed of knowledge
lies quiet in my mind.
Not growing in my heart.

I need the strength
to make the move.
The jump that takes me,
joyous,
to the richness of relationship with you.

Help me to want it, Lord.
Truly.
The rest will grow from that.

(No Strange Land, E. Askew, p. 83)

Alienation and inner renewal

31 We live in a hostile and fractured world. Everywhere we find a profound sense of alienation. We are alienated from God, hence the spiritual confusion and unreality that many experience. We are alienated from one another, hence broken marriages, violence on the streets and hostility between nations. We are alienated from the environment, hence the ravages of hunger, poverty, disease and pollution. We are also alienated from ourselves, hence the mental and psychological afflictions which cause distress in our lives.

... What is the answer to the tangle of human suffering that ensnares us all, one way or another? It is not education, since tragically the staggering technological progress made in the last few decades now threatens to destroy us all. Nor is it politics. New policies may change the structures of a nation, but until the heart of man is renewed nothing will be significantly different.

(*Fear No Evil*, D. Watson, pp. 105–106)

Finding the true self

32 Our age with its increase of leisure time has given itself increasingly to a quest for pleasure. Artificial risks are incurred in gambling, hunting, and racing. Artificial stimulation of the human body is produced by the use of stimulants and drugs. Vicarious entering into the experiences of others through reading of novels, dramatic presentations, cinema, and television make it possible to become aware of experiences without actual participation. All of this means that the ability to enter into life for one's self, to gain from it the deepest meaning, is forfeited by an endless quest for synthetic or substitute experience. No wonder there is an increasing sense of frustration, when days and years are dissipated in artificial living ... True joy can never be found in the artifacts of life but only in the achievement of fullness of being ... Fullness is never achieved by way of escape, substitution, or the use of vicarious experience. Fullness results from our finding the true self, and exercising the full potential of this true self.

(*Understanding Prayer*, E. Jackson, pp. 85–86)

THE RELIGIOUS QUEST

The importance of knowing God

33 Knowing about God is crucially important for the living of our lives. As it would be cruel to an Amazonian tribesman to fly him to London, put him down without explanation in Trafalgar Square and leave him, as one who knew nothing of English or England, to fend for himself, so we are cruel to ourselves if we try to live in this world without knowing about the God whose world it is and who runs it. The world becomes a strange, mad, painful place, and life in it a disappointing and unpleasant business, for those who do not know about God. Disregard the study of God, and you sentence yourself to stumble and blunder through life blindfold, as it were, with no sense of direction and no understanding of what surrounds you. This way you can waste your life and lose your soul.

(Knowing God, J. Packer, p. 15)

Life has meaning!

34 The words, 'I believe in God', are actually shorthand for a whole world of complex ins and outs, perhaps best summed up in two quotations which don't mention the word 'God' at all. The first is from Jung: 'Life is – or has – meaning and meaninglessness. I cherish the anxious hope that meaning will preponderate and win the battle.' The second is from Dag Hammarskjöld: 'I don't know who – or what – put the question, I don't know when it was put. I don't even remember answering. But at some moment I did answer yes to Someone – or Something – and from that hour I was certain that existence is meaningful and that, therefore, my life, in self-surrender, had a goal.'

(God for Nothing, R. MacKenna, p. 45)

Keeping a space for God in the silence of your heart

35 No one can find your meaning for you or walk into your silence. It must be done by you and can only be done if, in your heart, you believe you will not be left alone, and that through the darkness and silence there will come a wholeness and presence. We often run from such times of silence, we often panic at the thought of long, lonely stillness where we confront only our imaginings and fears. The ordinary mind boggles before the enormity of the proposition that God would bother to move in me and touch my boring ordinariness with himself: Most people are so overwhelmed by such lofty thoughts that they leave them to saints or theorists, to others better equipped for closeness to God.

(All Shall be Well, M. Meegan. p. 78)

36 The spiritual life demands a discipline of the heart . . . This doesn't mean, however, making things difficult for yourself, but making available the inner space where God can touch you with an all-transforming love. We human beings are so faint-hearted that we have a lot of trouble leaving an empty space empty. We like to fill it all up with ideas, plans, duties, tasks, and activities.

It strikes me increasingly just how hard-pressed people are nowadays. It's as though they're tearing about from one emergency to another. Never solitary, never still, never really free but always busy about something that just can't wait. You get the impression that, amid this frantic hurly-burly, we lose touch with life itself. We have the experience of being busy while nothing real seems to happen. The more agitated we are, and the more compacted our lives become, the more difficult it is to keep a space where God can let something truly new take place.

The discipline of the heart helps us to let God into our hearts so that God can become known to us there, in the deepest recesses of our own being. . . . Where God's heart speaks to your heart, there everything is made new.

(Letters to Marc, H. Nouwen, pp. 69–70)

Are we alone?

37 The question of life is so large, so overwhelming, that most of us content ourselves with the little pleasures of living, a quiet drink with friends, a pleasant meal, a stroll down Main Street. It is easier and much less painful not to look too far beyond the horizons of our situation. We try not to ask too many questions in case we might stumble accidently upon the answer . . .

From time to time our search for meaning becomes a thirst for immediate understanding. When one's mother or father is dying, or when one is close to death, a million thoughts and longings explode into one's mind. We need to talk, but so often there is no one there whom we can talk with, no one who speaks the same language. We grasp into the darkness and wonder – are we alone?

(All Shall Be Well, M. Meegan p. 36)

38 Religion endows us with the conviction that we are not alone in this vast, uncertain universe. Beneath and above the shifting sands of time, the uncertainties that darken our days, and the vicissitudes that cloud our nights is a wise and loving God. This universe is not a tragic expression of meaningless chaos but a marvellous display of orderly cosmos – 'The Lord by wisdom hath founded the earth; by understanding hath he established the heavens.' Man is not a wisp of smoke from a limitless smouldering, but a child created 'a little lower than the angels.' Above the manyness of time stands the one eternal God, with wisdom to guide us, strength to protect us, and love to keep us. His boundless love supports and contains us as a mighty ocean contains and supports the tiny drops of every wave. With a surging fullness he is forever moving toward us, seeking to fill the little creeks and bays of our lives with unlimited resources. This is religion's . . . eternal answer to the enigma of existence. Any man who finds this cosmic sustenance can walk the highways of life without the fatigue of pessimism and the weight of morbid fears.

(Strength to Love, M. L. King, p. 124)

39 The experience of finding meaning in existence comes from sensing that we are not isolated individual accidents in the universe, but that all living things share in an ultimate reality – Being itself, the act of being, which is active in every particular being: the absolute, unlimited life force which is in all beings – rather like the breath in the body – the soul.

(God for Nothing, R. MacKenna, p. 47)

40 Dear Lord – You are the Love that surrounds us,
              the Light that guides us,
              the Life that lives in us,
              the Hope that draws us ever onwards.

Amen

(J. Thompson)

41 The agony of human life is a compound of bodily pain, mental distress and emotional isolation even when in the closest company of one's peers. We are born lonely, for there is something of the soul that is sacred. It can never be satisfied with merely human company, for it remains unfulfilled, restless and strangely empty until it has attained the vision of God. The loneliness we all share, however oblivious of it we may be in the immediate thrust of workaday life, is unassuaged until we know God, who alone is constant and real.

(Gethsemane, M. Israel, p. 87)

It takes faith

42 To have faith requires *courage*, the ability to take a risk, the readiness even to accept pain and disappointment. Whoever insists on safety and security as primary conditions of life cannot have faith; whoever shuts himself off in a system of defence, where distance and possession are his means of security, makes himself a prisoner. To be loved, and to love, need courage, the courage to judge certain values as of ultimate concern – and to take the jump and stake everything on these values . . .

   Faith can be practised at every moment. It takes faith to bring up a child; it takes faith to fall asleep; it takes faith to begin any work. But we all are accustomed to having this kind of faith. Whoever does not have it suffers from overanxiety about his child, or from insomnia, or from the inability to do any kind of productive work; or he is suspicious, restrained from being close to anybody, or hypochondriacal, or unable to make any long-range plans. To stick to one's judgement about a person even if public opinion or some unforeseen facts seem to invalidate it, to stick to one's convictions even though they are unpopular – all this requires faith and courage. To take the difficulties, setbacks and sorrows of life as a challenge which to overcome makes us stronger, rather than as unjust punishment which should not happen to *us*, requires faith and courage . . .

To love means to commit oneself without guarantee, to give oneself completely in the hope that our love will produce love in the loved person. Love is an act of faith and whoever is of little faith is also of little love.

(The Art of Loving, E. Fromm, pp. 90–91)

43 Faith is my own private need of you reaching out to find you.
Faith is my own intelligence responding to yours.
My faith is my knowledge that in your vast intelligence you created this world – and me.
My faith is my growing conviction that you are not off somewhere running the universe, but here, now, with me.
That you care about me.
Thank you for this faith.

(I've got to talk to Somebody, God, M. Holmes. pp. 101–102)

Human beings 'walk in two worlds' – the material and the spiritual

44 Once you accept the existence of God – however you define Him, however you explain your relationship to Him – then you are caught for ever with His presence in the centre of all things. You are also caught with the fact that man is a creature who walks in two worlds and traces upon the walls of his cave the wonders and the nightmare experiences of his spiritual pilgrimage.

(*The Clowns of God*, M. West. p. 10)

45 There is a call in the silence that leads man to the fulfilment of his life. It leads one on from the trivial round of surface living in the company of those who are travelling along a well-worn way that returns to its point of departure, and reveals a more solitary uphill path away from the crowd. It is there that the inner voice of meaning declares itself. The voice may, of course, be disregarded. It is always disturbing those who would prefer to avoid a life of deep significance. But to those who are responsive, there is an abandonment of the world of ever-changing passions and fantasies and an entry into that timelessness of abiding reality which interpenetrates the world of form and gives it meaning.

The path towards an authentic life is also the path towards a knowledge of God. In travelling along this path one appears to live in two worlds, a world of spiritual reality in which the highest values are the measure of ultimate meaning, and an earthly world in which survival and satisfaction of the body are the most pressing concerns . . .

I soon became aware that my path was not, indeed never had been, random or fortuitous, but was being directed by a power far beyond the strength of my own will. To be sure, I had the choice of rejecting this higher direction, but as I grew more fully into a real person, so I accepted this higher impulsion and actively co-operated with it.

(*Precarious Living*, M. Israel)

46   Pilgrimage implies a journey. For me it means a commitment to search, to allow oneself to be led by God to the final union with him, which lies beyond death and which we call heaven . . .

Pilgrimage is adventure, is movement, travelling, sometimes knowingly in the right direction, at other times round in circles, blocking our own vision of the way with our need to be secure, comfortable and satisfied . . .

My commitment as a pilgrim is to the pilgrim God, who travels with His people, and is the destination of their travelling. It is wanting Him to make my heart so big that it will welcome all people, all experiences as signs of His speaking to me. The journey with this pilgrim God will lead me through experiences of cold, hunger, fatigue, thirst, emptiness, non-enoughness; it will also lead me through warmth, companionship, wholeness . . . glimpses of the God who is enough, who is everything for me.

Pilgrimage involves times of standing still, times of wondering, absorbing, praying, learning from all my experiences. It is time to recognise the 'giftness' of everything — from the daisy growing at my feet, to the star hurled mysteriously into the heavens . . . This essentially, is what makes of each day a journey, each day is a day of promise, a day of trust and faith, a day of setting out another step further along the way.

Death, for me, is the final step of the pilgrimage. It is that moment in my life where I will be totally alone in the presence of God, who will ask me, in the light of the quality of my pilgrimage through time, 'Are you ready to abandon absolutely everything and to trust me completely?' And then, I will reach 'home', that place from which I originally came. I will recognise God, my ultimate homeland, the end of all my travelling. He who has been with me along the way is there at the end . . . in my end shall be my beginning.

(Sr. B. Brent in *Religions and Education*, ed. A. Wood)

Religion and art

47 Consider this question: what is it that makes our species different from other animals? Here is one answer. We alone have imagination. We alone can conceive of things being different from the way they are. We alone can dream of new possibilities, can set about realizing them. We alone can be creative.

To possess imagination gives us the key to another world: the world of the spirit. To this flight of the creative imagination there is no limit: no limit to the infinite possibilities we may open ourselves up to.

And it is in this opening-up that we make the great discovery: we are not probing emptiness. The reality we meet is not indifferent to our search. We encounter another and greater creativity; this is a two-way affair. There is a positive, more mysterious resonance, not just the echo of our own cry. We find that cry to be part of a reality greater than ourselves.

(*The Mystery of Creation*, B. Lealman and E. Robinson, pp. 19–20)

48 The world we live in is full of problems. Most of these can, in the end, be solved. Or at least we can imagine solutions, even if we cannot achieve them.

But there are also mysteries: the everyday mysteries of birth and death; the mysteries of the unpredictable energies within the atom and of the endless expanse of space beyond us . . . the mysteries of human freedom, and of man's sense of good and evil in an apparently random world.

Such mysteries as these cannot be solved – for what would count as a solution? They can only be contemplated. And it is the contemplation of these mysteries that has given rise to religion – and to art.

A true work of art throws us back to reflect on our own encounter with life. It challenges us into daring to explore the mystery which lies at the heart of all religions, a mystery to which they all, in their ways, offer answers – answers, but no solutions.

(*The Image of Life*, B. Lealman and E. Robinson, pp. 3–4)

The need for religion

49 Religion is what happens when people explore the meaning of their existence; just as politics is what happens when people live together; and technology is what happens when people seek to solve material problems. Religious feeling is as necessary and inevitable among humankind as breathing, as is exemplified by the fifty-fold increase in the number of Chinese Christians during the anti-religious admiration of Mao Tse Tung.

That religion has been used as a reason for warfare and oppression is indisputable – but so have food, kinship, sex and natural resources; few would wish in consequence to abolish these. We need to understand the nature of man to explain why the world is screwed up – and *that* is a religious question.

(J. Garvey in *New Internationalist*, Dec. 1985, with minor changes)

50 If we go far enough asking 'How' and 'Why' we end up in the sphere of religion. 'Why do people behave the way they do?' 'Is it worthwhile struggling to help others?' 'Is history going anywhere?' 'Why has this happened to me?' These are all religious questions.

Some people seek answers to find a framework for ordinary living. It could be the day's news which sets them searching. For others it's a personal experience of loss or anxiety that is the driving force. Faced with a child's serious illness, parents will suddenly ask questions that have never troubled them before. They may cope with their personal tragedy through a faith which is big enough to interpret sickness and untimely death. On the other hand they may find nothing but an abyss of meaninglessness and then struggle to rebuild their lives around that perception. There is no way of proving which picture is true: both are 'faith positions' . . .

As people begin to probe the depths of meaning, religion acts as a kind of magnet on the soul. Whether you call it a story or a framework, people need something that helps them fit into a wider context than their own lives. So in every culture in history a form of religion has emerged alongside other developments in art or government.

(M. Hare Duke in *New Internationalist*, Jan. 1986, p. 12)

Religion is not an easy option but a quest for truth

51 It must, however, be acknowledged that every religion should carry a 'governmental health warning'. Instead of giving individuals or societies the courage to grasp new possibilities of letting go outmoded security, the name of God has been invoked on occasions against new thinking or social change. Religion has become a refuge for the frightened. Since frightened people also become vicious, repressive regimes and intellectual persecution have been justified as being faithful to the tradition. The danger comes when fidelity to a living god is equated with obedience to a fixed system of belief or morality.

(M. Hare Duke in *New Internationalist*, Jan. 1986, p. 13)

52 Unfortunately, religion can turn out to be the biggest cover-up job of them all – the ultimate comfort blanket. Freud said that you could account for the whole phenomenon of religious experience simply by looking at man's unconscious mind; you need look no further for the origin of God or gods than the fact that man is unable to cope with all the potential disasters and evils of life, and so he invents a benevolent figure who will probably shield him from harm in this life and then ensure his personal survival after death, preferably with lots of bliss thrown in. And this benevolent figure is none other than a huge blow-up of one's father – the original Big Daddy. If this is true, then religion must be a deeply retrogressive force in our lives, something that keeps us perpetually in a childish state. And there are certainly various pictures of God which fit this view, whether he is made the rubber stamp of approval for a plush lifestyle, a lucky charm, or the distant monarch on his throne, keeping careful tally of all the good little boys and girls.

Freud's views on religion are an important and helpful warning about the way religion can go off the tracks and become yet another retreat from reality. But they don't tie in very easily with the religion that is a quest for truth nor with the many, many people for whom belief, far from providing an easy ride, brings great hardship, putting them at odds with the state and leading to persecution.

(*God for Nothing*, R. MacKenna, pp. 38–9)

53 Religion is a life-long search, always incomplete. Even those who achieve a firm commitment to the Christian faith continue with many doubts, some beliefs being held more firmly than others. Always we are striving to understand more clearly, believe more strongly and behave more in accord with what we feel to be God's will ... No one can give us religion, manufacture our belief or change our behaviour for us. Fundamentally we must grow as persons towards God, and although many things external to us can help or impede our development, our religious growth is an individual and personal encounter with the divine.

(*Readiness for Religion*, R. Goldman, p. 11)

54 *[You can]* learn to accept and live with the realities of the situation — that life is infinitely complex, with no easy answers or black and white certainties; life is ambiguous, and almost all its accepted 'truths' are relative. You have to find your way with difficulty, and the religious life is not an arrival at a fixed point, but the starting of and sticking to a quest. The loss of certainty may be exactly the place where growth can begin, as we are forced to question and work out exactly what matters. As to the other question — 'So what?', 'Why bother?' — I'm not sure we can say anything helpful: 'Because you risk losing all that is most precious in our existence as humans'? or 'Because man isn't a sublimated ape but a repressed angel and the more you repress the restlessness of your spirit the nearer to being a sublimated ape you will become'? People have to find out for themselves, when their time of questioning comes. Pray God there's someone there then to be with them, who can give them space, silence and acceptance to help them on their way.

(*God for Nothing*, R. MacKenna, pp. 180–81)

Religion and science

It is often thought that religion and science are in conflict; yet Einstein, the most influential physicist since Newton, argued that 'Science without religion is lame' and 'Religion without science is blind.' Here he discusses his religious faith.

55 The most beautiful thing we can experience is the mysterious. It is the source of all true art and science. He to whom this emotion is a stranger, who can no longer pause to wonder and stand rapt in awe, is as good as dead: his eyes are closed. This insight into the mystery of life, coupled though it be with fear has also given rise to religion. To know that what is impenetrable to us really exists, manifesting itself as the highest wisdom and the most radiant beauty which our dull faculties can comprehend only in their most primitive forms – this knowledge, this feeling, is at the centre of true religiousness. In this sense, and in this sense only, I belong in the ranks of devoutly religious men.

(A. Einstein in *What I Believe*, ed. M. Booth, p. 27)

Another scientist, at one time a professor of Mathematical Physics at Cambridge, and now a clergyman, also sees science and religion as compatible.

56 Science and religion have to be regarded not as chalk and cheese but as cousins under the same skin. Both demand an act of faith, an honest attempt to test the truth by committing ourselves to the truth. To find out that truth some questions have to be asked: how big is the universe? Can there be any significance in the inhabitants of a speck of cosmic dust? What does it mean to say there is a Creator? Come to that, can a scientist believe in God? How will the universe end – in a bang, or a whimper or what? Is it all a tale told by an idiot or is there a meaning to it?

Someone might make Jesus the Lord of his life but is Jesus also the Lord of the starry heavens? These are questions that call for an answer but they are not like sums in arithmetic where the answers can be calculated. They are questions about how we understand the wonderful but strange world in which we live. To answer them calls for faith. That doesn't mean a leap in the dark hoping for the best, but a trusting belief, going beyond what can be proved but not beyond what is reasonable. Faith in this sense is essential to science – for example, faith that the world is orderly and that we can make sense of it. Faith in a similar sense is essential to belief in God. Science and religion must be seen as being compatible.

(*Signs of the Kingdom*, 'Faith', J. Polkinghorne)

57 The widespread assumption is that anything that cannot be proved scientifically is either meaningless and not worthy of serious consideration, or at least suspect and well avoided . . . It is worth stressing at this point that there are defined limits to the scope of science. Science essentially is descriptive in that it describes what can be seen or measured, but it cannot interpret what it sees or measures . . . Science cannot comment on the beauty of a sunset or on the love between a man and a woman. Such words as 'beauty' and 'love' are outside the language of science, but that in no way diminishes their reality. I heard of an entry in a communist textbook which defined a *kiss* as 'the approach of two pairs of lips with reciprocal transmission of microbes and carbon dioxide'. Tell that to a couple of lovers! As valuable as science undoubtedly is, there are vast stretches of reality which lie beyond its borders . . .

What is needed is . . . a widening of our world-view. We need an alternative world-view which embraces humbly all that science can offer and yet appreciates that there is more to come. It is like seeing the world with an extra dimension which in no way denies the other dimensions but presents another perspective.

(*Fear No Evil*, D. Watson, pp. 75–6, 79)

58 [*There is*] a widespread belief that there is a conflict between science and religion. But this is not true . . . Their respective worlds are different and their methods are dissimilar. Science investigates; religion interprets. Science gives man knowledge which is power; religion gives man wisdom which is control. Science deals mainly with facts; religion deals mainly with values. The two are not rivals. They are complementary. Science keeps religion from sinking into the valley of crippling irrationalism and paralyzing obscurantism. Religion prevents science from falling into the marsh of obsolete materialism and moral nihilism.

(*Strength to Love*, M. L. King, pp. 11–12)

Human nature is religious

59 Does it matter if belief in God gradually, or suddenly, dies in us? There are some who would regard it as a positive advantage, believing that it sets men free from a fantasy world and enables them to make a fresh start in a creative humanism. They believe that, freed from the shackles of religion, men would avoid the hideous bigotry which has inflicted such agony throughout the years. Released from watching the terrible perspectives of eternity, they would acquire a more adequate grasp of the time here available to them. They would be good without hope of reward, and without the appeal to their guilt which has been used to bludgeon them into decent behaviour hitherto.

Yet one could compile evidence to suggest that the nature of man is against them, that it is in our nature to be religious, just as it is in human nature to love, to act, to dance, to sing. Individuals may, for one reason or another, avoid these activities, certain groups may believe them so misguided or downright dangerous that they seek to discourage them, but nevertheless they assert themselves with regularity throughout human history. Man, the believer, may be as inevitable as man, the artist, using his energy fruitlessly when he tries to fight against this aspect of himself ... It is striking how consistently the longing for the Other has, throughout history, broken into every kind of society, even societies such as Soviet Russia where the State strove to educate people to believe that the Other is fantasy ...

In times of fear, suffering, or at the approach of death, it is not unusual for men to turn back to the Other ... After experiencing great pain or great isolation we often have the feeling that we have seen through the superficiality of our lives and perceived a great truth about the way things are. It is this kind of experience which brings individuals back again and again to the consciousness that religion has meaning, that it is not a deception nor a neurotic adjustment but that it is a part of them which may not be denied.

(*With love to the Church*, M. Furlong, pp. 11, 12)

60 It's fair to say the mainstream churches in North America and Europe have been fighting a rearguard battle for nearly 300 years . . .

By the early 1970s religion appeared to be making a comeback – in spite of hardening secular trends. Consumer culture offered the riches of the ages, but somehow it wasn't enough. According to American religion writer Harvey Cox, 'something had been lost; and what is lost seems to be religious: the sacred, the element of mystery in life, the transcendent, the spiritual dimension, a morality firmly grounded in revealed truth.' . . .

At the very deepest levels our spiritual needs seem as great as ever. Believers want a full-blooded religion that packs an emotional punch. One that provides both meaning and values for us to live by and that offers us a purpose beyond the bottomless hollow of consumer culture . . .

So where does all this leave us? In the end we still confront the same yawning void humankind has faced since the beginning. In the words of Cambridge theologian Don Cupitt 'we are still prompted to religious dread and longing by the thought of our own death, our own littleness, and the precariousness of human values in the face of Nature's vast indifference'.

We all confront these profound questions in different ways. Some of us are actively religious, many of us are not. Yet we all need faith in something – beyond the soul-destroying consumer culture that threatens to enervate us completely. The main thing we must do is take each other's faith seriously, whether it's faith in a better world or faith in God. It's time we dropped our arrogance and snobbery and began to see we're all in the same predicament.

But one thing we can't do is lose our critical edge. That's because religion cuts both ways. While faith *can* offer us a pathway to understanding the human purpose, religion has also sparked the worst of human passions – hatred, bigotry, intolerance, pride and bloodshed. When that side of faith surfaces we must be on our guard against religion and be prepared to speak out forcefully against it.

In the meantime, if we cannot agree on our approach to God, let's at least agree on our approach to the enemy: the rootless nihilism of the modern age.

('Flame of Faith' in *New Internationalist*, Jan. 1986, by W. Ellwood, pp. 8, 9)

Don't give up your search for God

61 Crossed Lines? . . . Engaged? . . .
'Hallo God, it's me again'
The adolescent agnostic
Yes, I know . . . one of the millions on earth.
Bother! line's engaged again!
Aren't I receptive enough to talk to him!
I suppose I'll have to wait patiently
Until I move on to a higher exchange!

Why won't he speak to me?
Is my mind too full of the refuse of worlds? . . .
(Perhaps the fault's a loose connection)
I can't even get a recording surface
To pass my message on
   'Hallo. God is out at the moment, but if you'll leave
your name and number . . .'
Not even an answering service
To . . .
   IS THERE . . .?
     . . . PROOF . . .
       . . . IS THERE? . . .
Must keep dialling
One day I'll get plugged in . . .
'Oh . . . Hallo, God . . . '
      Lynne Rees (17)

    (L. Rees (17) in *It's Important to Me*)

Belief and doubt

62 It's strange isn't it, how some people are religious and others aren't. For those who believe God is the most important fact in their lives. Everything comes to be bathed in this light. Yet other people seem to get by quite happily without it. Some religious people in the past used to accuse non-believers of being sinful. Of course no one is perfect, but this is obviously untrue if it implies that the non-religious are worse than the religious. There are good people with no religious faith, and horrible people who have faith and not much else . . .

Why some people believe and others don't remains a bit of a puzzle . . . Religious people say faith if a gift, and perhaps we get given this gift, or the opportunity to take it at different stages in our lives. For some the decisive period is during our teens when idealism can be at its highest. For other people it is middle age. Carl Jung noted that a very high percentage of his patients were middle-aged, and that the cause of their breakdown was fundamentally spiritual. For years before they had put all their energies into outward things, building a career or raising children, and now the neglected inner side was pushing through, often disturbingly.

(*Prayers of Hope*, R. Harries, pp. 18, 19)

63 Lord, even you know what it's like to feel as if 'God is
no more', to wonder if what you've staked your whole
life on is after all just an illusion.
You know what it is like to keep going in the dark by a
sheer act of will; to go on loving when there seems
to be no response; to abandon oneself to a divine
providence one can neither see nor feel.
Lord, when it's dark and we can't feel your presence,
and nothing seems real any more, and we're tempted
to give up trying, help us to know that you are
never really absent – that we are like a little child in
its mother's arms, held so close to your heart that we
cannot see your face, and that underneath are the
everlasting arms.

(by M. Dewey in *The One who Listens*, ed. Hollings and Gullick, p. 149)

64   The temptation of doubt puts our trust in God to the test. It can purify as gold is purified by fire. It can also cast a human being down into the bottom of a well. But there is still always a light shining from above. The darkness is never total. It never invades the whole person completely. God is present even in that darkness.

Harrowed by the trial of doubt, anyone who wants to live the Gospel allows himself to be reborn day after day by the confidence of God. And life finds meaning again.

Lord Christ, the meaning of our lives lies in your confidence in us. We tell you: 'Lord, I believe, come and help my lack of trust.' And you open for us a way of creation. Along this way, you show us how to create even with our own weaknesses.

>by Brother Roger in (*Meditations on The Way of the Cross*, Mother Teresa and Brother Roger, pp. 62, 64)

65   There seem to be quite a number of people about who would like to be fully believing Christians, but who don't feel certain enough about the truth of the Christian faith to really commit themselves to it wholeheartedly. They remain half-within and half-without; reluctant to give it up altogether, but uncertain about its basic truth. They want, and feel they ought to be able to have, greater certainty. We might put their point of view like this: God is meant to be the most important fact there is. If God is real and so important to us, then surely his presence ought to be inescapable? . . .

I would like to suggest that there is a very good reason why God does not make his presence obvious and inescapable. It has to do with leaving us free. Everyone knows how much we are affected by our environment and surroundings. If you mix with crooks all the time you are likely to end up a crook. If you climb a mountain and gaze across a whole range of mountains and valleys it is difficult not to have a sense of awe before such grandeur. The surroundings take hold of you. Now suppose we had been created in the immediate presence of God so that we were vividly aware of his reality all the time. What kind of freedom would we have? None at all. We would be like metal filings before a powerful magnet. So, it has been suggested, in order to leave us free, God created us at a distance from himself.

>(*Prayers of Hope*, R. Harries, p. 25)

Whom can we trust in times of need?

66 At times we may feel that we do not need God, but on the day when the storms of disappointment rage, the winds of disaster blow, and the tidal waves of grief beat against our lives, if we do not have a deep and patient faith, our emotional lives will be ripped to shreds. There is so much frustration in the world because we have relied on gods rather than God. We have genuflected before the god of science only to find that it has given us the atomic bomb, producing fears and anxieties that science can never mitigate. We have worshipped the god of pleasure only to discover that thrills play out and sensations are short-lived. We have bowed before the god of money only to learn that there are such things as love and friendship that money cannot buy and that in a world of possible depressions, stock market crashes, and bad business investments, money is a rather uncertain deity. These transitory gods are not able to save us or bring happiness to the human heart.

Only God is able. It is faith in him that we must rediscover. With this faith we can transform bleak and desolate valleys into sunlit paths of joy and bring new light into the dark caverns of pessimism.

(Strength to Love, M. L. King, p. 112)

67 A political prisoner, facing death, once wrote to his fiancée: 'I now realise why man, at certain times of his life, must descend into the depths. First, that he may learn to call upon and cry out to God; second, that he may recognise his own failings; and third, that he may undergo a change of heart.' . . . In the normal rush and hullabaloo of life, we have neither time nor mind for personal stocktaking. It is only when we are brought up short, when we are afraid or bewildered or disorientated, that we turn to God with an uncomprehending, frequently agnostic, cry for help. The bubble of our self-esteem has been pricked, our complacency has gone, and we are totally vulnerable. Then and only then can grace begin to operate in us, when we begin to take stock of ourselves, and to listen to our inner voices.

(Blessings, M. Craig, p. 142)

God is to be found at the heart of everyday life

68 A passage in Bishop Anthony Bloom's book, *School for Prayer*, tells of an old lady who came asking for his counsel: though she had prayed continuously for fourteen years she had never sensed the presence of God. How could she learn the secret? He gave her wise advice, and later she told him of her first experience. She had gone into her room, made herself comfortable, and begun to knit. She felt relaxed and noticed with content what a nice shaped room she had, with its view of the garden, and the sound of her needles hitting the arm-rest of her chair. And then gradually she became aware that the silence was not simply the absence of sound, but was filled with its own density. 'And', she said, 'it began to pervade me. The silence around began to come and meet the silence in me . . . All of a sudden I perceived that the silence was a presence. At the heart of the silence there was Him.'

The fascination of that account lies in the woman's simple recognition that her awareness of God came together with her deeper awareness of the familiar things around her. It must always be so. The Holy Spirit is the invisible third party who stands between me and the other, making us mutually aware . . .

The Holy Spirit is that power which opens eyes that are closed, hearts that are unaware and minds that shrink from too much reality. If one is open towards God, one is open also to the beauty of the world, the truth of ideas, and the pain of disappointment and deformity. If one is closed up against being hurt, or blind towards one's fellow-men, one is inevitably shut off from God also.

(*The Go-Between God*, J. Taylor, pp. 18–19)

69 In all crucial matters of responding to the Kingdom we have to be ready to wait ... to wait in awesome silence upon him with eagerness and expectancy.
Waiting upon God is not a waste of time, like 'kicking one's heels'! A full and undivided waiting upon God leads to a disclosure from him of his holy will ...

Take time to think – it is the source of power
Take time to play – it is the secret of perpetual youth
Take time to read – it is the fountain of wisdom
Take time to pray – it is the greatest power on earth
Take time to love and be loved – it is a God-given privilege
Take time to be friendly – it is the road to happiness
Take time to laugh – it is the music of the soul
Take time to give – it is too short a day to be selfish
Take time to work – it is the price of success
Take time to do charity – it is the key to heaven.

(*Pilgrimage*, J. Smith-Cameron, p. 57)

70 How can we move to a knowledge of God, Who alone can fill us with that meaning in life which makes all difficulties appear as nothing compared with His radiance? The answer is simple. It is by living in awareness of the moment and responding positively to the challenge of relationships with those around us. This is the basis of spirituality. It is no longer to be thought of as something reserved only for those who have dedicated their lives to silent contemplation in a religious community. The dedication is as fundamental as ever, but in the contemporary scene we have to participate actively in and partake wholeheartedly of every episode of the passing scene of life.

It is in the depths of the living mass that we glimpse the mountain of transfiguration. The journey downwards into our own inner nature is also the way to God. Nothing is valueless to him who can discern the divinity that manifests itself in all its creation.

In this realised divinity there is eternal joy.

(*Summons to Life*, M. Israel, p. 15)

71 We find God, not divorced from the world, but intimately part of it. We find him in a face, in a moment of music, in the long haul of daily chores, in the street, in the most unexpected and common of places. We find him in the heights of the heavens and in the depths of our doubting hearts, in the world's confusion and noise, and in the bright darkness of inner prayer.

Holiness lies in accepting the tenderness of God making divine the most mundane, making special the most ordinary. The sacred is when the smallest action done with care and compassion, no matter how unimportant it may seem, is done as a hymn, as a gift, as a promise of a new life in a new creation, and the dawn of that creation is us.

(*All Shall Be Well*, M. Meegan, pp. 133, 139)

72 So many of us flee from people crying out in pain,
people who are broken.
We hide in a world of distraction and pleasure
or in 'things to do'.
We can even hide in various groups of prayer
and spiritual exercises,
not knowing that a light is shining
in the poor, the weak, the lonely and the oppressed . . .
Yes, in that broken child,
a light is shining;
in that man in prison,
a heart is beating;
in that woman, victim of prostitution,
there is a yearning for life;
in the rich and greedy person, seeking power,
there is a child of purity;
in that young man dying of Aids,
there is the light of God;
in every human person, no matter how broken, sinful,
hardened, dominating or cruel,
there is a spring of water waiting to flow forth.

(*The Broken Body*, J. Vanier, pp. 1–2)

God is made visible in loving actions

73 Now I would like to tell you something very important about the way to make God's presence visible in our life.

A pity I discovered it too late!

I have behaved like the man who travels over mountains and seas to look for a treasure, then returns home exhausted and discovers to his surprise that the treasure is in his house.

There you are: God is in your house.

In my house, in your house, in Mother Teresa's house in Calcutta . . .

As He is a hidden God no-one sees Him, but everyone seeks Him because everyone longs to see Him . . .

But while I'm thinking about the best way of discovering God, of seeing God, and while you're studying the problem, Mother Teresa goes out into the streets and sees someone dying alone and without help. She does not rationalize about God, or work out a five-year plan, or theorize about mankind.

She comforts the dying man, she gets help to carry him into the house, she gives him water to drink, she combs his hair, she wipes away his deathly sweat, she thinks to herself with tenderness 'I want him to die knowing a friend is near.' Not at all an ambitious programme, not a revolution, just a true act of love.

Brothers, confronted with Mother Teresa the world stands still for a moment: it sees God passing down the streets of Calcutta . . .

And you can carry on.

God reveals himself where there is anyone who respects life, who desires the light, who seeks to love. Every time you open yourself to life, every time you act the truth, every time you love, God is there in your action.

It is as if you were creating your God.

And this is why I said that God is within things
within events
within your gestures of love.

By doing things as Jesus would do them, as God would do them, you free God from the veils of invisibility and make him visible on man's journey.

Faith is an act, not a series of idle remarks.

Hope is an undertaking bathed in light, not a pious sentiment.

Charity is an event, not a devotional little prayer.

(*The Desert in the City*, C. Carretto, pp. 95, 96)

The voice of God speaks in creation

74 Lord, in my short and hurried day
May I pause for long enough to touch a leaf,
Or breathe the fragrance of a flower.
And in that moment
May I be in quiet communion.
With your endless, life-giving love.

(from 'The Silent Witnesses' in *Lord of my days*, F. Topping, p. 38)

75 For St Francis of Assisi . . . the sun and the moon, fire and water, the human body and all of reality spoke of God. The smallest particle of creation was a theophany, a revelation of God.

The ordinary Christian seldom has this kind of vision. His act of seeing is a mere seeing which stops at appearances and does not go in to the meeting. He needs eyes to read the wind, the stars, people's faces, in such a way that he sees more than what appears.

But there *are* moments which stand out from all the others, moments which come like a gift, moments when the focus shifts and a single leaf becomes a universe, a rock speaks prophecies and a smile transforms a relationship. We call such moments sacred, because in them we glimpse something of the sacredness of life, the wonder of God. They are sacramental moments which act as telescopic lenses on life, enabling us to see more than we normally do, making present to us a world that is not always perceived.

(J. Conway)

76   In such a place I could not speak
For leaf and lichen declared this holy ground,
A sanctuary.
Sweet chestnuts were falling,
Green, prickly spheres
Bursting apart on leaf-layered earth.
Acorns, pale and immature,
Spattered the ground around the oak.
My shoes depressed
The rain-soaked moss and glistening grass,
Footsteps hushed in the stillness of the trees.
Until, passing through
I came into the open
And like a rich symphonic chord falling on the ears,
My eyes were assailed with colours that sang
Chromatic scales of gold, and yellow and amber.
Leaves of brown and red and green
Raised praise to their creator
For the gift of deep and mellow autumn

And it was lavish,
As the love of God always is.
This nature is his nature,
Extravagantly generous.
Like autumn leaves his blessings fall
And all creation
Acknowledges the love that never dies.

(from 'An Autumn Prayer' in *Lord of my days*, F. Topping, pp. 42, 44)

In April 1989, ninety-nine Liverpool supporters were crushed to death, and another four hundred injured, at Hillsborough football ground in Sheffield. The Bishop of Stepney reflects on the response to this disaster by those who attended a special service on the Liverpool football ground at Anfield.

77   In his autobiography, Arthur Miller describes a childhood visit to the synagogue with his great-grandfather. At one point in the worship, the old man took off his shoes to reveal naked white feet. He then made Arthur cover his eyes and forbade him to look. Then began a thumping and a bumping and deep voices all singing their own individual song. In

the end the boy *had* to peep – and there was the unbelievable sight of his great grandfather and the other old men having a wonderful time singing and dancing before the Lord. He quickly shut his eyes again, but the effect on him was profound. He had been at the edge of a mystery which was sacred and puzzling.

Reading this of the young Arthur Miller I was reminded of generations of Russians who have kept their sense of mystery and God alive, because their grandmothers had secret icons in their bedrooms, where flickering candles lit up the haunting holy face of Christ or His mother.

Looking back on my own childhood, I don't remember ever being given a sense of mystery. Everything had to be explained. Perhaps, without realizing, I met the great God when I climbed the rocks or watched a stag cross a combe. But no one helped me glimpse the sacredness at the heart of our life. Religion was portrayed as something to learn about, not a God to encounter.

I was thinking this was not just my story, but the story of many of us in post-war Britain. Maybe the faculty for mystery died somewhere. Perhaps that accounts for the appeal of Africa and India, because the sense of the sacred is so alive there. School Chapel, Mattins and Evensong, didn't open me to that mystery. But then God touched me and awakened the idea that we are surrounded by the beauty of eternity. So when I stood by the ocean, or watched our child born or knelt in a place steeped in centuries of prayer, they carried the mystery of God. When we experience the holy, we see through our fingers to the edge of God's reality.

If we have no shrine, no inner reverence, nothing that makes us catch our breath with wonder, then we close a door. I am convinced that the grotesque lack of respect for others in our society, its pornography and violence, grows where nothing is sacred.

A priest friend who has spent these days in Liverpool and Sheffield said that the atmosphere at Anfield was like a Cathedral, youngsters praying and people standing in reverence. It made me think that perhaps we would not have been plunged into the years of hooliganism and violence, if reverence had been the starting point rather than the aftermath.

(Radio 4's *Thought for the Day*, Bishop J. Thompson, 19 April 1989)

Coming to know God

78 We only come to a knowledge of God at all in so far as we are capable of growing out of our self-centredness and are willing to live before one who, by definition, makes a total difference to our lives. The knowledge of God is rarely overwhelming and inescapable. For most people there is only a flickering, dawning awareness which is always related to our willingness to know and love God. In this way God preserves our freedom and ensures that the pilgrimage we make is our own journey.

(*Evidence for the love of God*, R. Harries, pp. 5–6)

'Dwell secretly in the presence of God'

79 The initial reaction of someone who has a really personal encounter with Jesus is not to start shouting it from the rooftops but, rather, to dwell secretly in the presence of God. It is very important for you to realize that perhaps the greater part of God's work in this world may go unnoticed. There are a number of people who in these days have become widely known as great saints or influential Christians; but the greatest part of God's work in our history could well remain completely unknown. That's a mystery which is difficult to grasp in an age that attaches so much value to publicity. We tend to think that the more people know and talk about something, the more important it must be. That's understandable, considering the fact that great notoriety often means big money, and big money often means a large degree of power, and power easily creates the illusion of importance. In our society, it's often statistics that determine what's important: the best-selling LP, the most popular book, the richest man, the highest tower-block, the most expensive car. With the enormous growth of advertizing it's become nearly impossible to believe that what's really important happens in secret.

Yet . . . we do have some intimations of this. A human life begins in the seclusion of the womb, and the most determinative experiences occur in the privacy of the family. The seedling grows in the seclusion of the soil, and the egg is hatched in the seclusion of the nest.

(*Letters to Marc*, H. Nouwen, pp. 66–67)

God's 'still, small voice'

80   A score of years ago a friend placed in my hand a little book which became one of the turning points of my life. It was called *True Peace*. It was a medieval message, and it had but one thought, and it was this – that God was waiting in the depths of my being to talk to me if only I would get still enough to hear his voice.

I thought this would be a very easy matter, and so I began to get still. But I had no sooner commenced than a perfect pandemonium of voices reached my ears, a thousand clamouring notes from without and within, until I could hear nothing but their noise and din. Some of them were my own voice, some of them were my own questions, some of them were my prayers. Others were the suggestions of the tempter, and the voices of the world's turmoil. Never before did there seem so many things to be done, to be said, to be thought; and in every direction I was pushed and pulled, and greeted with noisy acclamations of unspeakable unrest. It seemed necessary for me to listen to some of them, but God said, 'Be still, and know that I am God.' Then came the conflict of thoughts for the morrow, and its duties and cares; but God said, 'Be still'.

And as I listened, and slowly learned to obey, and shut my ears to every sound, I found, after a while, that when the other voices ceased, or I ceased to hear them, there was a still, small voice in the depths of my being that began to speak with an inexpressible tenderness, power and comfort. As I listened, it became to me the voice of prayer, and the voice of wisdom, and the voice of duty, and I did not need to think so hard, or pray so hard, or trust so hard, but that 'still, small voice' of the Holy Spirit in my heart was God's prayer in my secret soul, was God's answer to all my questions, was God's life and strength for soul and body, and became the substance of all knowledge, and all prayer, and all blessing; for it was the living God himself as my life and my all.

This is our spirit's deepest need. It is thus that we learn to know God; it is thus that we receive spiritual refreshment and nutriment.

(*Silence* by J. Southall, pub. Religious Society of Friends)

Conversion experiences

81 Right down the line I was Mr Average, sticking to a kind of ingrained convenient-enough moral code, but with no inclination whatever to take it further.

After all, why should I? Life was fabulous. At twenty-one, I was being paid for the only thing I ever wanted to do, the fans were screaming, and career-wise I had it made. Endless opportunities in films, television and recording were opening up. If it was lonely at the top, I couldn't imagine why; around me were people I liked, friends I worked with, and family I loved and lived with.

And then, very very faintly, something inside said, 'Please, I'm not satisfied'.

I don't know really what sparked it off, although I usually put it down to my father's death. He'd been ill for about six months and during that time our relationship changed quite drastically. A heart condition forced him, for the first time, to depend on other people . . . His death, from a thrombosis, after being in hospital for two or three weeks, was a shock. I was really quite shattered and subconsciously it may have triggered off much more than I realised. All I am sure of is that about six months after he died I was working in Australia and, for the first time in my career, felt absolutely empty. Outwardly nothing had changed: audience raction was still as fervent; friends were as friendly, but somewhere something was missing. On stage it was fine, the same total enjoyment and elation, but afterwards a kind of classic anticlimax . . .

The crunch came at a Whitsun camp in Lewes and, for the umpteenth time, I was doing verbal battle with Bill over some issue that had cropped up in one of his talks. By then we'd become very good friends but on this occasion I felt really annoyed by one of his questions: *'How do you know you're a Christian?'*

It was a fair, relevant and necessary question and, with hindsight, I'm thankful he asked it. Faced with the same question before, I'd always waffled out an answer but at that Whit camp my hackles went up because for the first time it dawned on me that I couldn't honestly answer it. I knew Bill could; he would talk about a personal relationship with Christ and a day when, as a schoolboy, he consciously committed his life to Christ. But for me there was no relationship, no assurance – just a package of second-hand dogmas.

A few weeks after that camp I became a Christian. Appropriately enough, it was at Bill's house in Finchley. I was staying there throughout the filming of 'Finders Keepers' at Pinewood Studios, and one evening I read the words of Jesus in the book of Revelation: 'Behold, I stand at the door and knock; whoever hears my voice and opens the door, I will come in.' The only way I can explain it is that that must have been God's moment for me, because, although I'd been through it all in my mind many times before, I only realized then that a relationship was a two-way thing and I'd contributed nothing.

So, in that front bedroom in Finchley, I lay on the bed and mouthed a very hesitant prayer. It was something like: 'All right, Jesus, I'm aware that you're knocking – you'd better come in and take over.' It was nothing more complicated than that. No flashes of light, no voices in the ear, no sudden visions. All I recall is that I meant what I said and was willing for the consequences.

People often knock or try to explain away Christian conversions as emotional illusions which never wear off. Now I happen to be pretty familiar with my emotions. Like a lot of stage people, I'm what you'd call an emotional kind of person. At a weepy film I'll be through my third tissue before most of the audience have finished their choc-ice. If anyone's vulnerable to emotional pressure, it's me.

That's why I know what I'm talking about when I say that what happened that evening was nothing to do with emotional jiggery-pokery. It was a decision not prompted by a temporary mood of a hellfire sermon, but by a cool and reasoned-out conclusion – arrived at after months of hassle – that I needed Jesus.

(*Which One's Cliff?*, C. Richard, pp. 64, 65, 72–3)

82 It was almost midnight. The day had been unexceptional and I can remember nothing in particular occupying my mind. I had already gone to bed and the light was out. Suddenly, I was overtaken by an unshakable conviction that I was not alone. The person with me was not physical, though it seemed so. I was being confronted by God.

How could this be? I was a nominal Christian and went to church sometimes. But I'd never been sure about God. Now there was no doubt. With heart pounding I knelt by my bed – it seemed the right thing to do – and said 'God, I know you are real and I know you want me. But I don't know what for and I don't know where it might lead. However, I cannot now deny you and cannot have peace of mind until I place myself in your hands. So take me.'

Knowing that I had done what was required I got back into bed and fell asleep with feelings of excitement mixed with peace. That was 16th June 1961 in my University lodgings. Since that time God has led me along routes I'd never dreamed of; not always routes I wanted but always routes which proved to be the best. In retrospect I don't regret any of the journeys I've been constrained to travel. It's not a case of logic. It wasn't logical that I should be called to be an Anglican priest when I wasn't even an Anglican! I've not operated on logic, but on the conviction that the step I am about to take is the right one, or I'll be prevented from taking it. That's Christian adventure – anything but dull!

God doesn't have a production line for Christians. We're all different and find our own route to faith. I was lucky to undergo a sudden change so all doubt was dispelled. Others tread a steadier route as they make progress towards their conviction that God is.

('No God – No Peace – Know God – Know Peace',
M. Johnson, *The Trident*, March 1989)

The power of the Bible to convert

83 The words of Scripture are still able to speak to individuals with a simple self-authenticating power. I would like to cite the experience of . . . Antony Bloom, now archbishop to the Russian Orthodox Church in Britain. While a student in Paris he had lost his faith. Under pressure he went in a surly manner to hear a lecture on Christ and Christianity. The rest must be told in his own words:

> I hurried home in order to check the truth of what the lecturer had been saying. I asked my mother whether she had a book of the gospels because I wanted to know whether the gospel would support the monstrous impression I had derived from this talk. I expected nothing good from my reading, so I counted the chapters of the four gospels to be sure that I read the shortest, not to waste time unnecessarily. And thus it was the gospel according to St Mark which I began to read. I do not know how to tell you what happened. I will put it quite simply and those of you who have gone through a similar experience will know what came to pass. While I was reading the beginning of St Mark's gospel, before I reached the third chapter, I was aware of a presence. I saw nothing. I heard nothing. It was no hallucination. It was a simple certainty that the Lord was standing there and that I was in the presence of him whose life I had begun to read with such revulsion and such ill-will.
>
> (*Why Pray?*, M. Gibbard, p. 90)

'The quiet assurance of an inner voice'

Martin Luther King is helped to face the hostility which ultimately led to his assassination.

84 After a particularly strenuous day, I settled in bed at a late hour. My wife had already fallen asleep and I was about to doze off when the telephone rang. An angry voice said, 'Listen, nigger, we've taken all we want from you. Before next week you'll be sorry you ever came to Montgomery.' I hung up, but I could not sleep. It seemed that all of my fears had come down on me at once. I had reached the saturation point.

I got out of bed and began to walk the floor. Finally, I went to the kitchen and heated a pot of coffee. I was ready to give up. I tried to think of a way to move out of the picture without appearing to be a coward. In this state of exhaustion, when my courage had almost gone, I determined to take my problem to God. My head in my hands I bowed over the kitchen table and prayed aloud. The words I spoke to God that midnight are still vivid in my memory, 'I am here taking a stand for what I believe is right. But now I am afraid. The people are looking to me for leadership, and if I stand before them without strength and courage, they too will falter. I am at the end of my powers. I have nothing left. I've come to the point where I can't face it alone.'

At that moment I experienced the presence of the Divine as I had never before experienced him. It seemed as though I could hear the quiet assurance of an inner voice, saying, 'Stand up for righteousness, stand up for truth. God will be at your side forever.' Almost at once my fears began to pass from me. My uncertainty disappeared. I was ready to face anything. The outer situation remained the same, but God had given me inner calm.

Three nights later, our home was bombed. Strangely enough, I accepted the word of the bombing calmly. My experience with God had given me new strength and trust. I knew now that God is able to give us the interior resources to face the storms and problems of life.

(*Strength to Love*, M. L. King, pp. 113–14)

GOD

Believing

85 So where is man headed? In a sense, to ask questions about the nature of man is also to ask questions about meaning; to ask, 'What am I here for?'. To look at life and one's experience of humanity may lead to saying, 'It's all a sick joke' ... or may lead one towards God-talk. In this case to say 'I believe in God' would, when unscrambled, mean that I don't think my life feels like an accident in the universe, and that in my life and my experience of other people I have sensed that behind human life there is a power which is most fully expressed in the human personality and which is utterly trustworthy.

(God for Nothing, R. MacKenna, p. 49)

86 The first time I can remember having difficulty with believing in God was while I was a theological student. My own unbelief resulted from a genuine misunderstanding of psychology. I was quite taken in by the suggestion that men believe in God as Father only because their subconscious desires create and project for them a father-figure in order to give some kind of security in this bleak, everchanging world. This figure, I was then convinced, had no objective reality. It was like a mirage of water which thirsty travellers think they see in a desert. It did not at that time occur to me that psychology, just because it has deliberately limited its field of study to the human personality, does not investigate any reality apart from ourselves. Psychology may well explain how we come to desire a father-figure, but psychology itself cannot tell us whether or not there is a Being with fatherlike care for us.

(Why Pray?, M. Gibbard, p. 47)

Making God in our image

87 We were created in God's image, yet we relentlessly search for a God who will manage to fit our image, a God who will find a slot in our lifestyle, who will agree to let us hold on to the things we depend on. We talk to him half heartedly just in case he might by chance be there. The honest search leads us towards a different language, a strange language which is hard and difficult to learn in a modern world. It is the language of the saints. It was spoken before creation and is the deepest language of the human heart, the mystery of inner silence.

(All Shall Be Well, M. Meegan. p. 77)

88 To some degree we all create God in our own image. Hopefully, we've left behind the nice-old-gentleman-with-a-white-beard, but we each hold a picture in our minds. Perhaps of a merciful God, or a judgemental one: a father, a brother, or a lover. Some suggest we should think of God as mother. Whatever the picture, we tend unconsciously to select and arrange our experiences of life to confirm the image we already hold. We neatly file away and forget the signs that tell us the disturbing news that God is bigger than our ideas. Yet he is not to be confined in the little box of my prejudices, or the straitjacket of my timidity.

Maybe it would be more comfortable if he were. Holding on to God is sometimes a bit like holding an elephant by the tail — you have to go in his direction, not yours. And his direction leads to expanding horizons: . . . 'for as the heavens are higher than the earth, so are my ways higher than your ways and my thoughts than your thoughts' (Isaiah 55:9).

(No Strange Land, E. Askew, p. 54)

Can we prove God?

89 There is no *proof* that God is real – if by 'proof' we mean the way it can be proved that this book exists or that 2 + 2 = 4. God (if real) is just too big to be fitted into that kind of proof. And even if you make up your mind that God is real, you will never 'know' this in the way that you can know the truth of a formula in chemistry or a fact in the newspaper . . .

There is a kind of proof which you can have when thinking about God – and a kind of knowledge, too. It is the knowledge that you have when you say you 'believe' in a friend. It is the proof that you have when you love someone else and find yourself loved back. That love is proved to you deep down, although someone looking on can say: 'They don't really love each other – I see no proof.' And deep down you *know* the person you love, although someone looking on can say, 'I can't see what he sees in her.' Your relationship with God can become like that. You still will not have complete certainty, but you will have enough confidence to decide that for all practical purposes you are prepared to bet your life that God is there.

(*What Anglicans Believe*, D. Edwards, pp. 10–11)

The limitations of God-talk

90 No words, however pure or sacred, will fully describe God . . . For God can never be pinned down like a dead butterfly, reduced to a formula or reproduced in a photograph. No talk about God can be completely accurate, because all such talk must use words which were invented to describe the world or man – not God. Like shots which always miss their target, human words will always fall short of the glory of God. But the words can show in what direction the glory lies; however imperfectly, they can point to the reality. For example, when we say that God is 'personal' we must remember that he cannot be a person as we are people. He must be much more. But the word 'personal' points to the reality that, if he is real, God cannot be *less* than personal – for he cannot be less than us.

(*What Anglicans Believe*, D. Edwards, p. 10)

Evidence of God

91 The fact remains, however, that our total human understanding is both finite and limited. God, if he exists at all, is an infinite God and infinitely greater than the finite circle of our understanding. We would all be incurably agnostic unless God had broken through that circle in ways that we can understand. It is the Christian conviction that God has done precisely that: through *creation*, which shows us the power of God, through *conscience*, which shows us the goodness of God, through the *scriptures*, which show us the wisdom and justice of God, but supremely through *Jesus of Nazareth*, who was the Son of God and the living revelation of God on earth. Here is something our minds can grasp concerning the truth of God. 'He who has seen me has seen the Father,' said Jesus. If we want to know what God is like, we start with Jesus. Even here we cannot know the total truth of an infinite God, for that would be impossible for our finite mind, but we can know truths that are important.

(*Fear No Evil*, D. Watson, p. 77)

92 Christianity cannot be proved. It can only be witnessed – by Christians. By men and women who have, over two millenia, found in Christ the neighbour they need, the saviour they sought, the light that illumines the whole landscape of reality and makes them say, 'It is good to be here.'

(*Reflections*, H. Lavery, p. 14)

God or Materialism?

93 God, I now believe, dynamically interpenetrates the universe. That is, he is actively present in all persons and things though, of course, in very different degrees or modes. He is the spring of life, and he is what holds all things together in existence.

Many people find it difficult, I know, to accept this, but the alternative seems to me to be sheer materialism, that is to say that basically matter alone is real. Neither of these two alternative interpretations of the universe, I grant, can be proved. In my opinion, we ultimately have to choose between them. In the end, our life style will show which we have chosen.

For me, of these two alternatives, the dynamic divine interpenetration of the universe seems to raise fewer difficulties than materialism. I run the risk of over-simplification, but it seems to me that if we accept sheer materialism we take all depth out of aesthetic experience. For example, an evening's music would then be only the setting in motion of sound waves and the corresponding vibration in our eardrums, and that would be all. In the same way, all depth of meaning would, I think, be taken out of our most treasured personal relationships. For lovers the deepest and most understanding making of love would then be reduced to physical and chemical changes in the human body, and that would be all there was to it.

(Why Pray?, M. Gibbard, p. 17)

94 The Holy Spirit [is] that unceasing dynamic communicator and Go-Between operating upon every element and every process of the material universe, the immanent and anonymous presence of God ... But if the Holy Spirit were confined, as it were, within the continuum of progressive evolution we could never know him or consciously experience him. We do not experience the growth of cell structure in our own bodies, unless it has become malignant, nor are we aware of the beating of our own hearts unless for a short period something brings it to our attention. In the same way, our conscious recognition of the Holy Spirit comes to us not through the ceaseless pressure of his presence upon us but at particular moments of encounter which he initiates.

(The Go-Between God, J. Taylor, p. 64)

Evolution witnesses to the existence of God

95 Many things about your life, about man's life on the earth, and about the universe, are indeed hard to explain if there is no God and therefore no good purpose running through it all. Atheism has its problems ...

Why does anything exist, rather than nothing?

If the universe is nothing more than an accident, how has it happened that it contains so much order and so much beauty? It has been said that it works like a machine, yet sleeps like a picture.

The machinery of evolution can be understood. There are many mutations (genetic changes), and out of these the fittest – those best adapted to the struggle for life – survive. So chance comes into it. But does the whole process consist of nothing more than chances which are selected by the iron necessities of life? Is the universe merely a lottery or a Bingo hall? If so, how has it happened that there has been such amazing progress? How has sheer chance produced Shakespeare and Beethoven, Einstein and Rembrandt?

(*What Anglicans Believe*, D. Edwards, pp. 13–14)

96 We look at the evolution of man. If it is all a matter of chance, why is there this steady process upwards? The more we look at the world and at man, the more we feel that chance appears to be only another name for purpose, because if chance is the moving force, then chance has achieved what mind and purpose would have achieved. I think that it is more difficult to believe in a chance which can produce order than in a mind which did produce it.

(*Testament of Faith*, W. Barclay, pp. 39–40)

God is Creator

97 When my son was very young he asked if we would give him a picture of God for his birthday. That flummoxed us. But my wife and I talked, and we decided that the only thing for us to do was to buy him a beautiful map of the world. So we brought him a map which had little pictures all over it, to show what the different countries were like in terms of their creatures and culture and architecture. We hung it over his bed, and for several years he was confused between God and the world.

Some people would have accused us of pantheism. But what we were struggling with was what is now called pan-en-theism – the idea that God is perceived and understood in all of his creation. He isn't that creation, but he is the force within it.

('A Picture of God' by P. Challen in *My World*, ed. S. Brown, p. 97)

98 To envisage creation in terms of life-giving energy and inspiration is a far profounder insight than the earlier image of God the potter or builder who remains outside and essentially separate from his handiwork . . . If we think of a Creator at all, we are to find him always on the inside of creation. And if God is really on the inside, we must find him in the processes, not in the gaps. We know now there are no gaps, no points at which a special intervention is conceivable. From first to last the process has been continuous. Nature is all of a piece, a seamless robe. There is no evidence of a break, as we once imagined, between inorganic matter and the emergence of the first living organisms; nor between man's animal precursors and the emergence of man himself. If the hand of God is to be recognized in this continuous creation, it must be found not in isolated intrusions, not in any gaps, but in the very process itself.

(*The Go-Between God*, J. Taylor, pp. 26, 28)

God is just

99 [*Bible texts*] regard judgement and condemnation as an essential counterpart of salvation: talk of heaven is incomplete until a word has also been said about hell. God's love is misunderstood if it is not balanced by God's justice.

It would seem, then, as if the theme of judgement is not in opposition to the theme of love. On the contrary, it is suggested, without judgement love would be trivialized. A God defined only in terms of love would have no muscle. The definition would fail to spell out the burning passion that love is, and the demands it makes on both lover and beloved. Can a God who only loves, and never passes judgement, be taken seriously? Does he not inevitably become a benign uncle who smiles indulgently on the children as long as they are happy? All sense of the awesomeness of God – of his holiness, as the Bible calls it – would be lost. So would all sense of the enormity of evil, as if it did not really matter, and could easily be forgiven . . .

If the dark themes must continue to form part of the Christian message, it is to draw men's attention to the seriousness of human history. Evil continues to be a dimension of that history, even in the lives of good people and no one should imagine it is of little account. It has the demonic power to reduce the world to the chaos out of which the Creator God originally rescued it.

Yet that creative act of God is the foundation of our hope. The love which overcame the primal darkness, which drew a living universe out of nothing and a living Christ out of the tomb, is stronger than all the powers of evil. The eternal lovelessness of hell may be a perfect image of what we can achieve by our own unaided efforts. But it cannot be a description of any sort of reality that will actually come to be, because it leaves out of reckoning the power of love.

(*Death And After*, H. Richards, pp. 56, 78–9)

God is eternal

100 When we speak of God's eternal or everlasting life . . . we should not be thinking of how (infinitely) long it lasts. The word may be clumsy, but it is trying to say something about the quality of God's life, not the quantity. God lives a life which, by definition, is free of all the restrictions with which we know our own lives beset. Not only the restrictions of time, but all the other limitations we experience, of incompleteness, mediocrity, impoverishment, superficiality, shabbiness, constraint, instability. God's life is complete, full, rich, deep, glorious, free, unwavering.

Such is the life we all yearn for. And we could not yearn for it if we had not, in our best moments, already tasted something of it. There is no one who has not experienced, even if only minimally, how full and rich life can be. In such experiences, even time becomes an irrelevant factor. It is not that we had much more than our usual share of it. On the contrary, the experience may, in terms of time, have lasted only for a short while. But while it lasted, we were no longer conscious of time. We realized that time is only one of the dimensions we live in, and that we can live in dimensions which can't be measured in hours or years, even if they were multiplied to infinity. We experienced the timelessness of eternity because we managed, if only for a while, to live as God does, totally in the present tense.

(*Death and After*, H. Richards, pp. 43–4)

God is love

101   God is Love: let heav'n adore him;
    God is Love: let earth rejoice;
Let creation sing before him,
    and exalt him with one voice.
He who laid the earth's foundation,
    he who spread the heav'ns above,
He who breathes through all creation,
    he is Love, eternal Love.

God is Love: and he enfoldeth
    all the world in one embrace;
With unfailing grasp he holdeth
    every child of every race.
And when human hearts are breaking
    under sorrow's iron rod,
Then they find that selfsame aching
    deep within the heart of God.

God is Love: and though with blindness
    sin afflicts the souls of men,
God's eternal loving-kindness
    holds and guides them even then.
Sin and death and hell shall never
    o'er us final triumph gain;
God is Love, so Love for ever
    o'er the universe must reign.

    (God is Love, no. 32 by T. Rees in *100 Hymns for Today*)

102   If God is Love, we can catch glimpses of Him in our daily lives, through our loving relationships. The writer of the First Letter of John tells his readers:
'Dear friends, let us love one another, for love comes from God. Everyone who loves has been born of God and knows God. Whoever does not love does not know God, because God is love.'

    (J. Thompson, quoting from 1 John 4: 7–8, N.I.V.)

103 The most important thing you can say about God's love is that God loves us not because of anything we've done to earn that love, but because God, in total freedom, has decided to love us. At first sight, this doesn't seem to be very inspiring, but if you reflect on it more deeply this thought can affect and influence your life greatly. We're inclined to see our whole existence in terms of *quid pro quo*; you scratch my back, and I'll scratch yours. We begin by assuming that people will be nice to us if we are nice to them; that they will help us if we help them; that they will invite us if we invite them; that they will love us if we love them. And so the conviction is deeply rooted in us that being loved is something you have to earn. In our pragmatic and utilitarian times this conviction has become even stronger. We can scarcely conceive of getting something for nothing. Everything has to be worked for, even a kind word, an expression of gratitude, a sign of affection . . .

When we know that God loves us deeply and will always go on loving us, whoever we are and whatever we do, it becomes possible to expect no more of our fellow men and women than they are able to give, to forgive them generously when they have offended us, and always to respond to their hostility with love. By doing so we make visible a new way of being human and a new way of responding to our world problems.

Whenever, contrary to the world's vindictiveness, we love our enemy, we exhibit something of the perfect love of God, whose will is to bring all human beings together as children of one Father. Whenever we forgive instead of letting fly at one another, bless instead of cursing one another, tend one another's wounds instead of rubbing salt into them, hearten instead of discouraging one another, give hope instead of driving one another to despair, hug instead of harassing one another, welcome instead of cold-shouldering one another, thank instead of criticizing one another, praise instead of maligning one another . . . in short, whenever we opt for and not against one another, we make God's unconditional love visible; we are diminishing violence and giving birth to a new community.

(*Letters to Marc*, H. Nouwen, pp. 49, 54, 55)

104 It is scarcely surprising that the encounter of the human soul with the very spirit of love should have effects beyond our wildest imaginings. Yet we are surprised. We are surprised because we lack faith in the tremendous reality of the sheerly spiritual. Earth-bound and material-minded, we are reluctant to surrender to the appeal of anything we cannot touch or see . . . We murmur 'God is love'. But, whilst we appreciate the power of love in human affairs, we seem incapable of raising our sights to contemplate the mere possibility of such a power increased to infinity.

(*The Prayer of Jesus*, T. Corbishley, p. 29)

105 In my medical experience as well as in my own life I have again and again been faced with the mystery of love, and have never been able to explain what it is . . . Whatever one can say, no words express the whole . . . I do not use it in its connotations of desiring, preferring, favouring, wishing, and similar feelings, but as something superior to the individual, a unified and undivided whole. Being a part, man cannot grasp the whole. He is at its mercy. He may assent to it, or rebel against it; but he is always caught up by it and enclosed within it. He is dependent upon it and is sustained by it. Love is his light and his darkness, whose end he cannot see . . . Man can try to name love, showering upon it all the names at his command, and still he will involve himself in endless self-deceptions. If he possesses a grain of wisdom, he will lay down his arms and name the unknown by the more unknown . . . that is, by the name of God.

(*Memories, Dreams, Reflections*, C. Jury, p. 387)

God the Trinity

106 It is in our relationship with God that we most need a doctrine of the Trinity. We can relate to him as Father, or as Son, or as Holy Spirit. We may perhaps unconsciously relate more easily to one than to another.

To many people – possibly most – God is essentially the Father. The Lord's Prayer is addressed to him. The requirement that we should become as little children seems to fit such a relationship.

The difficulty in relating to God the Father is partly the difficulty of imagining him – of forming an image. To me the best image is that of the air 'in which we live and move and have our being.'

The advantage of being able to relate to the Son is that we need have no difficulty in imagining Jesus Christ in the flesh. Having a common father, it is possible to think of Jesus more as a brother – as someone with whom we are on Christian name terms . . .

The Holy Spirit is probably the least easy member of the Trinity to relate to *as a person*. The image of the dove is not very helpful. But the Holy Spirit, unless we shut him out, has no difficulty in relating to us . . . The love wherewith a man loves God or his neighbour is the Holy Ghost. It is not the *work* of the Holy Ghost only: it *is* the Holy Ghost.'

('The Holy Trinity' by I. Dunlop in *Church Times*, p. 9, June 26, 1987)

God the Holy Spirit

107 What makes a landscape or a person or an idea come to life for me and become a presence towards which I surrender myself? I recognize, I respond, I fall in love, I worship – yet it was not I who took the first step. In every such encounter there has been an anonymous third party who makes the introduction 'acts as a go-between, makes two beings aware of each other, sets up a current of communication between them. What is more, this invisible go-between does not simply stand between us but is activating each of us from inside . . .

I have already started to talk about this force of influence in very personal terms. I am bound to do so because the effect of this power is always to bring a mere object into a personal relationship with me, to turn an *It* into a *Thou*.

So Christians find it quite natural to give a personal name to this current of communication, this invisible go-between. They call him the Holy Spirit, the Spirit of God. They say that this was the Spirit which possessed and dominated the man Jesus Christ, making him the most aware and sensitive and open human being who has ever lived – ceaselessly aware of God so that he called him, almost casually, Father, and fantastically aware of every person who crossed his path especially the ones no one else noticed.

The objective fact that men everywhere and in every age have experienced this overwhelming encounter with him who is both within and beyond them deserves the most serious and thorough examination.

(*The Go-Between God*, J. Taylor, pp. 16–17, 65)

108 Jesus did not deny that he was possessed. A fire burned strong within him and many were warmed by its affection and brushed by its holiness. He did not hoard this Spirit; he gave it away. Totally. And those few who have received this Spirit do not say so. They have no need. They also give it away as a tree drops its generous fruit for human refreshment. These fruits are many and they are various. Fine things like love and joy and peace . . .

Every age sees itself as uniquely catastrophic; many become dispirited and some desperate. The defeatist is a man possessed by negation, who has lost heart and hope and sees no possibility of reprieve or redemption . . .

Yet there is another spirit contending for possession of the heart and this spirit will not surrender to adversity. Its symbols are wind and fire, primordial things and not of human manufacture. This spirit lives in contest with all that is lifeless, all that is loveless. It animates – that is its genius. In a man or woman it is evident in courage and a refusal to take cover in cynisism. In a society it is evident in its power to harmonise. It can still conflict and heal division. It is a spirit of wholeness, of holiness, and releases a sick society from deadness and from divide . . .

But spirit is not at our command. It is the given, the God-given, and its proper verb is 'receive'. All we can do is receive the Spirit. For the Spirit is always abroad, endlessly blowing, but the timid heart resists its invasion. The Spirit is only for the receptive, for those whose hearts are open, whose eyes are alert, whose attitude remains one of wonder.

(*Reflections*, H. Lavery, pp. 34, 35–36, 37–38)

109 Saint Paul tells us that a life nourished by the Holy Spirit
is like a tree which bears good fruit.
'The fruit of the Spirit is love, joy, peace,
patience, kindness, goodness,
faithfulness, gentleness and self-control.'
God's Spirit is the source of our life,
so may we bear much fruit.
Amen

(J. Thompson, quoting *Galatians* 5: 22–23, N.I.V.)

God the Father

110 Jesus *shows* us God in the only way we can understand – in a human life. He doesn't hand out statements *about* God. He himself makes God present to us . . . What, then, does the life of Jesus *tell* us about God? If you read the Gospels certain things stand out. Jesus forgives sinners; he heals the sick; he is compassionate; he is patient; he restores people to life; finally he gives his own life in love.

So the God Jesus shows us is a forgiving God, a compassionate God, a God who heals, a patient God, a life-giving God and, above all, a loving God. If we believe in Jesus we can no longer think of God as a remote, authoritarian God-in-the-sky. This God disappears for ever. Jesus shows us another face of God. His word for God is 'Father'. And his relationship with the God he calls Father is one of warmth, familiarity and love . . .

This doesn't only change our image of God. It changes our image of *ourselves*. We are not miserable slaves of a mighty and ruthless king. We are children of a loving God whom Jesus tells *us* to call 'Father'.

And what does it mean to be a child of God?
The life of Jesus answers that question too. He shows us how someone who is perfectly in tune with God lives. He is not fearful, timid or anxious. His relationship with God is a mature relationship. He is not divided within. He knows who he is, and he faces the demands life makes on him without dithering. He is true to the message of life he proclaims. In short, he shows us what it means to be fully human and fully alive. He is the perfect picture of a true human being . . .

So Jesus wasn't so much concerned with telling us what to *do*. He was much more concerned with showing us who we *are*. And his mission wasn't so much to make us more religious. It was to make us more alive!

(*How to survive being married to a Catholic*, R. Gallagher and M. Henesy, pp. 12–13)

God the Son

111   It was often thought that God was up above us. The ancient Egyptians thought that God was the sun up in the sky. The Sumerians built temple-towers on their plains so that they could be nearer their gods. The ancient Greeks thought the gods lived on top of Mount Olympus which reached up into the clouds.

We still speak of God up above us, today. The first person into space was a Russian called Yuri Gagarin. He reported back to earth that he couldn't see God anywhere up there! It is obviously silly to take this picture literally, and yet it still has much to say to us, for when we think of God above us we are expressing *his* greatness and our *own* humility.

Christianity doesn't deny that God is high and mighty, but it is unique in that it also believes that God came down to our level – that he became a human being, Jesus Christ. That he understands, from the *inside*, what it is like to be human. One Christian creed even states that 'he descended into hell' – there is no level that God cannot penetrate.

So when we find ourselves in the depths of despair or sadness, when we are degraded by our own failures, or when we are just feeling low – then we are assured that God is there with us – within reach – closer to us than our own breathing, and that he can raise us up.

(J. Thompson)

112   'No one has ever seen God;' writes St John, 'it is the only Son, he who is nearest to the Father's heart, who has made him known.' And he has made him known in the only terms we can understand: in human terms, as the man Jesus Christ. His every word and action is radiated by his knowledge of the Father . . . Jesus knows the Father to be wholly Love, and that to be reconciled to God is to be caught up into 'a love that will not let us go'.

(*A Year Lost and Found*, M. Mayne, p. 53)

113 What the New Testament claims is that Jesus cannot be properly understood unless in saying his name you say 'God': and that neither can God be known, not properly known unless in saying his name you say 'Jesus'. And that neither can be known unless you use the word 'Love' . . .

But we need to walk a little warily here. To say that 'God is like Jesus' is not to say that 'Jesus is like God'. The latter would mean that the One whose glory no man can look upon and live, the God of Gods and the Lord of Lords, is reduced to human dimensions, and that cannot be so. But to say that God is like Jesus is to believe that the One whom we call God chose to reveal as much as we need to know of his nature in the only terms we can understand.

(*A Year Lost and Found*, M. Mayne, pp. 54–55, 56–57)

114 So then for me the supreme truth of Christianity is that in Jesus I see God . . .

It is not that Jesus *is* God. Time and time again the Fourth Gospel speaks of God sending Jesus into the world. Time and time again we see Jesus praying to God. Time and time again we see Jesus unhesitatingly and unquestioningly and unconditionally accepting the will of God for himself. Nowhere does the New Testament *identify* Jesus and God. Jesus did not say: 'He who has seen me has seen God.' He said: 'He who has seen me has seen *the Father*.' There are attributes of God I do not see in Jesus. I do not see God's omniscience in Jesus, for there are things which Jesus did not know. I do not see God's omnipotence in Jesus for there are things which Jesus could not do. I do not see God's omnipresence in Jesus, for in his days on earth Jesus could only be in one place at any given time. But in Jesus I see perfectly and completely and finally, and once and for all revealed and demonstrated, the attitude of God to men, the attitude of God to me. In Jesus there is the full revelation of the mind and the heart of God. And what a difference it means to know that God is like that!

(*Testament of Faith*, W. Barclay, pp. 49–50)

The love of God in Jesus Christ

115 In the gospel, it's quite obvious that Jesus chose the descending way. He chose it not once but over and over again. At each critical moment he deliberately sought the way downwards . . . Even though he was full of divine power, he believed that changing stones into bread, seeking popularity and being counted among the great ones of the earth were temptations.

Again and again you see how Jesus opts for what is small, hidden and poor, and accordingly declines to wield influence. His many miracles always serve to express his profound compassion with suffering humanity; never are they attempts to call attention to himself. As a rule, he even forbids those he has cured to talk to others about it. And as Jesus' life continues to unfold, he becomes increasingly aware that he has been called to fulfil his vocation in suffering and death. In all of this, it becomes plain to us that God has willed to show his love for the world by descending more and more deeply into human frailty.

(*Letters to Marc*, H. Nouwen, p. 39)

116 But Jesus Christ does not only change our idea of what God is and what we might become: he also changes our idea of what love is. For 'the love of God in Jesus Christ our Lord' is not a love which is soft and yielding and emotional. This love is diamond-hard and costly: it is a giving of yourself to others; it is a refusal to hate, whatever the cost; it is a refusal to be moved from what you know in your heart to be good and true and right. Love is quite often a kind of dying. It demands obedience and loyalty, and it may well encompass anguish, pain and even death.

(*A Year Lost and Found*, M. Mayne, p. 55)

117 In one sense He was always an outsider to the world, in another He was the worldly man *par excellence*. He was born and died an outsider: born outside the normal conventions of child-birth – 'no room at the inn', died outside the normal conventions of decent dying – on a cross outside the city walls; he never conformed to the world's expectations – He did not stick close to His family, He did not observe his position in society, He lived a rather beatnik sort of life with no settled home, accepting hospitality where He could get it with graciousness and naturalness, in no way feeling under any obligation to those who gave it. He had no hesitation in challenging those in authority, He was very careless of those with whom He associated, He had no worry about His reputation when an ex-tart joined his followers, nor did it worry Him that people might think He was homosexual by going round with a group of men and letting John lean on His breast at supper. In all these ways He was an outsider.

But yet He was at home with all men: at the age of twelve He could mix naturally in the temple with a group of scholars; He could equally accept the hospitality of Simon the Pharisee, of Zacchaeus the publican; He could promote the gaiety of a wedding by providing extra wine when they had already well drunk; He could share the feelings of Martha and Mary when their brother had died: He could give great gifts of healing to the twisted spirits crying out for integration; He could receive without embarrassment gifts for Himself of costly ointment to cleanse His road-dusty feet. He could speak naturally to complete strangers without having to be introduced; He could be at home with fishermen, tax-collectors, tarts, learned men, scribes, religious leaders, Jews and Romans. He could speak with dignity and on equal terms without arrogance to the High Priest and to the Roman Governor; He could afford to ignore with dignity King Herod. He could speak with equal love on the Cross to soldiers, to a dying criminal, to those who jeered at Him, as to His Mother and His best friend: yet that same love could be sufficiently detached to enable Him without compunction to leave his home and family and to make no distinction within the group of disciples between those He felt special affection for on closer intimate terms and the others.

(*Prayer in the Secular City*, D. Rhymes, pp. 66–7)

Jesus was true to himself

118 He had the 'courage to be'. Never in the whole course of the Gospel story do we get the impression of one who was putting on an act, adopting a pose, trying to live up to other people's expectations of Him. He was at home in the most amazing diversity of surroundings because he was just Himself. He played no role, He had no self for one situation, and another self for another situation.

(Prayer in the Secular City, D. Rhymes, p. 65)

119 Here was a man who lived his life in response to the call of love. To be true to his call, to the journey set before him, he risked alienating friends and family and overturning the accepted religious beliefs of the time. He was open to everyone he met, without side or prejudice. If he felt that someone needed a good kick in the pants to shock him out of his self-righteousness, he was only too happy to oblige; if a prostitute needed to know that she was loved and accepted for herself as a person, not as a piece of flesh, then he gave her that acceptance regardless of the raised eyebrows and the scandalised religious. He gave his followers a startlingly new vision of authority, based on humility and service, and in the service of his mission to mankind he was faithful until death – a death whose keynote was complete forgiveness, love returned for hatred . . .

What did he *do*, exactly? Well, he was. He existed. He was real. Wherever humans went, he went – he didn't hang around the temple moaning to God about how awful they were or polishing his halo. Jesus cured and cared by being himself with people, not by playing a part. And in the end he challenged the world to search for the meaning of life by laying down his own for love, as a servant. He preached, wandered, visited, told stories, chatted, argued, drank, went on picnics and to dinner parties, touched, prayed, wept, doubted, suffered, agonised, died – he lived to the full his own destiny, true to God and to himself.

(God for Nothing, R. MacKenna, pp. 90, 128)

120 Jesus is the Word – to be spoken.
Jesus is the Truth – to be told.
Jesus is the Light – to be lit.
Jesus is the Life – to be lived.
Jesus is the Love – to be loved.
Jesus is the Joy – to be shared.
Jesus is the Peace – to be given.
Jesus is the Bread of Life – to be eaten.

Jesus is the Hungry – to be fed.
Jesus is the Thirsty – to be satiated.
Jesus is the Naked – to be clothed.
Jesus is the Homeless – to be taken in.
Jesus is the Sick – to be healed.
Jesus is the Lonely – to be loved.
Jesus is the Unwanted – to be wanted.
Jesus is the Leper – to wash his wounds.
Jesus is the Beggar – to give him a smile.
Jesus is the Drunkard – to listen to him.
Jesus is the Mentally Ill – to protect him.
Jesus is the Little One – to embrace him.
Jesus is the Blind – to lead him.
Jesus is the Dumb – to speak to him.
Jesus is the Crippled – to walk with him.
Jesus is the Drug Addict – to befriend him.
Jesus is the Prostitute – to remove from danger and befriend her.
Jesus is the Prisoner – to be visited.
Jesus is the Old – to be served.

(Mother Teresa in *Meditations on the Way of the Cross,* Mother Teresa and Brother Roger, pp. 23–4)

LOVING OTHERS

1 Corinthians 13

121 In his first letter to the Corinthians (chapter 13), Paul created an unforgettable portrait of Jesus Christ – and of the true Christian. It is the portrait of a man who has found his life after apparently losing it because he is so unselfish. He has found his life, because he has found what love can do. 'Love is patient, love is kind and envies no one. Love is never boastful, nor conceited, nor rude, never selfish, not quick to take offence. Love keeps no score of wrongs; does not gloat over men's sins, but delights in the truth. There is nothing love cannot face; there is no limit to its faith, its hope, and its endurance.'

Rightly, that description of love is one of the most popular parts of the Bible. What has been said so far is, however, not the full Christian understanding of love. The advice to treat other people as we should wish to be treated if we were in their shoes is known as the 'golden rule' and it is given in the Bible. But the Bible says much more.

The Bible shows that to believe in love is *to trust in the power of love*. It is to act in the conviction that love will find a way and win through. So many other things seem more immediately attractive than true love ... But to believe in love is to say that true love is the most valuable, the most satisfying and most glorious experience in life. It is to say that here is gold – and the rest is bogus. So many other things seem more powerful than love. Violence often does. Aggressive argument often does. But to believe in love is like expecting a great river to flow into the sea. You trust love to win through because it is the mightiest force, the most dynamic energy, in the universe.

(*What Anglicans Believe*, D. Edwards, p. 50)

122   Lord, you have taught us
That love is patient and kind,
That love is never pleased
When others make mistakes;
But love looks for and rejoices in goodness.
Love does not want to expose faults.
Love always believes the best;
For love is always hopeful, always patient,
Love never gives up.
Teach me Lord
To make all my judgements
In the light of the love that never dies.

(Lord of my days, F. Topping, p. 59)

123   Even if I am clever and brilliant and have a great way with words and have no love, something in me is cold and empty.

And if I devote my life to the service of the poor and give all I have to feed the starving, and lay down my life, but have no love, then what's the point?

Love endures all things, Love suffers long, it is always kind. Love is not jealous, Love is not out for display, it is not conceited or unmannerly, it is neither self-seeking or irritable.

Love does not take account of any wrong that is suffered, it sees no joy in injustices, but comes from truth.

Love bears everything in silence and has indomitable faith. Love hopes in every situation no matter how hopeless, and it endures without limit.

Love never fails, everything else in life will pass away . . .

Now we see unclearly, only in part. Then, we shall see him face to face . . . We will understand just as now we are understood.

Then after everything is gone and has passed away, there will only be three things left,

Faith, hope and love, and the greatest of these is love.

(All Shall Be Well, M. Meegan, pp. 142–43)

'The love of God operating in the human heart'

124 The meaning of love is not to be confused with some sentimental outpouring. Love is something much deeper than emotional bosh. Perhaps the Greek language can clear our confusion at this point. In the Greek New Testament are three words for love. The word *eros* is a sort of aesthetic or romantic love. In the Platonic dialogues *eros* is a yearning of the soul for the realm of the divine. The second word is *philia*, a reciprocal love and the intimate affection and friendship between friends. We love those whom we like, and we love because we are loved. The third word is *agape*, understanding and creative, redemptive goodwill for all men. An overflowing love which seeks nothing in return, *agape* is the love of God operating in the human heart. At this level, we love men not because we like them, nor because their ways appeal to us, nor even because they possess some type of divine spark; we love every man because God loves him. At this level, we love the person who does an evil deed, although we hate the deed that he does.

(*Strength to Love*, M. L. King, p. 50)

125 Dear God of Love –
It's not easy to love as you would have us love:
It's not easy to forget myself and put others first;
It's not easy to become so involved with other people
   that I think only of their welfare;
It's not easy to love those people who are always around –
   I take them so much for granted;
It's not easy to form a real relationship with the people
   I just meet casually during the day;
It's not easy to love people I've never met –
   the nameless millions I hear about in the news.
Lord, it's not easy to love.
But help me to realise that LOVE is a temendous force
   in which I can share – if I really believe in it;
That LOVE is strong enough to change my life,
to transform the world . . .

(J. Thompson)

126 It is not easy to become part of the body of community.
To do it, we must die to ourselves,
to our pride,
to our need to do our own thing,
and to our desire to be recognized as unique
and all-important.
It is a struggle to give others their proper place,
free from judgement, condemnation or envy.
It is difficult to accept the differences of others
especially when their temperament, their make-up,
is totally different from ours.
Different types of people
seem to oppose or contradict each other.
Perhaps even more threatening
are those people who reflect back to us
those parts of our being we cannot face or accept.
They reveal to us
the brokenness that we deny in ourselves.
In a special way, they become our enemies.

Yet each one has his or her place in the body.
And Jesus calls us together to form one body,
to love one another as he loves us.
He calls us to live the miracle of love and of grace
which is community:
one body, one faith, one shepherd.
Not a community where everyone is the same,
not a community where there is fusion
   (which frequently means confusion),
but a community where, inevitably, on the human plane
and on the plane of our psyches,
there is tension and pain,
and feelings of dissatisfaction.
A community must be built on faith
and in the belief that we have been called into one body.

(*The Broken Body*, J. Vanier, pp. 101–102)

127 To love is to open our hearts to people
to listen to them,
to appreciate them
and see in them their own unique value,
to wish deeply that they may live and grow.
To love is to give our lives for one another.
It is to forgive,
and to be compassionate.

(*The Broken Body*, J. Vanier, p. 37)

Giving and getting

128 An English woman who went to help at Mother Teresa's Mission in Calcutta, as a medical worker, had this to say:

Those who go to work should be prepared to 'give their all'; but in the end they will find they have gained more than they gave. This theme recurs throughout a book she has written on the work of the Missionaries that she saw when she was in India. The book is called Love Until It Hurts, a title which comes from something Mother Teresa said:

We must love Christ with undivided love until it hurts. It must be a total surrender, a total conviction that nothing separates us from the love of Christ. We belong to Christ.

In her book, Daphne Rae says this:

True joy is one of the greatest gifts of life . . . Joy is not confined to the Religious or 'do-gooder', but it comes to those who in a sense forget themselves and become totally aware of the other.

And she finishes the book with these words:

I have found the paradox that if I love until it hurts, then there is no hurt, but only more love. As I held and fed the morsel of life that was an aborted baby; as I held the hand of a man dying from cancer and felt his trust and gratitude; I could see – feel – touch God's love which has existed from the beginning. The Kingdom of God, I realised, is within reach of everyone, and is to be found in the love we bear one another.

(*Love Until It Hurts*, D. Rae)

'When I was hungry . . .'

Jesus said: 'Whatever you did for one of the least of these brothers of mine, you did for me.' *(Matthew 25:40)*

129 When I was hungry, you gave me to eat.
When I was thirsty, you gave me to drink.
Whatsoever you do to the least of my
   brethren, that you do unto me.
Now enter the house of my Father.
When I was homeless, you opened your doors.
When I was naked, you gave me your coat.
When I was weary, you helped me find rest.
When I was anxious, you calmed all my fears.
When I was little, you taught me to read.
When I was lonely, you gave me your love.
When in a prison, you came to my cell.
When on a sick bed, you cared for my needs.
In a strange country, you made me at home.
Seeking employment, you found me a job.
Hurt in a battle, you bound up my wounds.
Searching for kindness, you held out your hand.
When I was Negro, or Chinese, or white and
Mocked and insulted, you carried my cross.
When I was aged, you bothered to smile.
When I was restless, you listened and cared.
You saw me covered with spittle and blood,
You knew my features, though grimy with sweat.
When I was laughed at, you stood by my side.
When I was happy, you shared in my joy.

(Mother Teresa in *Meditations on The Way of the Cross*, Mother Teresa and Brother Roger, pp. 18–19)

Made in the image of God

130 I shall always remember visiting Mother Teresa's Home for the Dying in Calcutta and being shown round by the sister-in-charge, Sister Luke. The dying lie on thin palliasses of straw, the men in one section of the extended ward, the women and children in the other. Between the two wards is a small cubicle with a plastic curtain drawn across the front of it. Just before I reached the home an old woman had been brought in from the streets in a filthy condition. She was barely recognisable as human.

'Come and see,' said Sister Luke, and took me across to the curtained-off trough. She drew back the curtain. The trough was filled with a few inches of water, in which was lying the stick-like body of the old woman. Two Missionaries of Charity were gently washing her clean and comforting her at the same time. Above the trough, stuck to the wall, was a simple notice containing four words: 'The body of Christ'. It is an image I can never forget.

(*A Year Lost and Found*, M. Mayne, p. 69)

131 A friend of mine has rheumatoid arthritis, and when it was at its worst her husband would push her round in a wheel-chair. People would then smile kindly at her, but address their questions to her husband. 'How is she . . . ?', they would ask him. Since the disease had affected her hips and not her head she found this treatment enormously irritating.

Society does this sort of un-personing all the time. Not just to a person who is in a wheel-chair but to any person who is different. A disabled person and an old person will often suffer from the indignity and so will a poor person. Then there is the person who for one reason or another some sections of society look down on or disapprove of . . .

But every person in the whole world is still a human being made in the image of God, however damaged they are by sickness or by sin, and whether it is their fault or someone else's. If we will dare to look into their eyes we shall hear the cry of their heart: 'I'm a person too . . .'

(*My World*, ed. S. Brown, p. 31, passage by editor)

Meeting the needs of others without imposing our own solutions

132   Lord, can I hear what they are saying?
For 15 years now I've been working for development;
I've tried to understand the complexities of world trade,
the injustices of the tea and coffee industry;
soft loans and hard loans,
the rescheduling of debts
— to say nothing of the aid target of 0.7 percent of the GNP . . .
I've struggled through the Brandt Report,
pored over the plans for the new economic order.
Development, we called it: World Development,
our efforts to help the rest of the world catch up
with our western values, industry, education, health.

Can they mean it, those Christians in Asia,
that development is not their word, not on their agenda?
'Recognition' is *their* word.
Recognition of *their* way of life,
their view of land and family,
their language, their culture.
'We want to be recognised as human beings,
free to be what we want to be,
with the right to shape our own destiny
in our land.'

Lord, forgive me,
I thought that I was helping,
but I was so blinded by my own culture
   that I could not see theirs;
so proud of my own language that I taught that,
   instead of learning theirs;
so wrapped around by love of my own immediate family
that I could not imagine such love committed to their extended family;
so sure of right and wrong, in western terms,
   that I could not recognise them
in the perspectives of another society.

People of Asia, Africa, Latin America and the Caribbean,
forgive us.
Often when we suggested a solution to your problems,
we were removing your freedom to find your own way through.
Often when advice poured in from outside
   it sapped your will to achieve results from inside.
Often when we took on responsibility
   we were taking it away from you.
Often when we used our power to help
we were implying that you could not help yourselves.

Must we, in our day, learn
with Martha
that it can be more blessed to receive than to give?
with Mary
the gift of listening, recognising Christ.

('Development is not our word', by D. Temple in Network, U.S.P.G. magazine, July 1986, p. 9)

In spite of our differences, each of us is a person

133   Often when I have spoken on race and colour to audiences in this country, I have begun by saying: 'Now you have a choice of terms. We can either speak about "black" people and "white" people or we can speak about "coloured" people and "colourless" people. Which one do you want to use?' Invariably the audience choose black and white. I think this is because although a person might not mind being considered 'white', he or she would not want to be 'colourless'!

I do this to point out that both groups of people see themselves as normal. Black and white are both colours, and that's that. But when you describe one group as 'white' and the other group as 'coloured' (which is not a colour) you are suggesting that anything other than white is a deviation from normal. Incidentally, I always insist on repeating the word 'people'. So we have unemployed *people*, not 'the Unemployed'; elderly *people* not 'the Elderly'; homeless *people*, not 'the Homeless'; black *people*, white *people*, disabled *people* and so on. We need all the help we can get to remind ourselves and others that in spite of differences, we are all *persons*. That is a profound theological statement.

It is easier for some of us to see this than for some other people. If like me you have grown up in the Caribbean where there is a mixture of various ethnic groups, a person's colour tells you as little about his intelligence, ability or humour as do his clothes! . . .

But there are many people who haven't had the experience of living in a multi-ethnic society. Until recently if you grew up in England you wouldn't have had any real or first-hand experience of black people. What you felt about them would largely depend on your cultural norms and what your history and geography books (written by white people) said about them. So you would be ignorant without knowing that you were ignorant, because for a number of vested-interest reasons, black people were normally projected as sub-human. Europeans who exploited Africa and inflicted degrading conditions of slavery and slaughter upon fellow human beings could only retain an image of themselves as civilized by pretending that black people were not human!

I wish I could say that all this was now behind us, but I remember a television programme which showed a young American soldier who had been serving in Vietnam paying a visit to his old school and being welcomed by flag-waving adoring children. He told them that he was out there fighting for freedom. He said: 'Vietnam is a lovely country. The one thing that is wrong with it is the people. They are not like us. They don't feel pain as we do . . .'

('Colourless and Coloured' by W. Wood, in *My World*, ed. S. Brown, pp. 53-4, 55)

Friendship

134 Friendship is what we all need, long for and hope for. It is what causes the greatest joy in our lives, and can also cause the greatest hurts. In friendship we share secrets with another, develop loyalties that are often intense and make relationships that sometimes last long through our lives. It may mean moments of just being together, of shared humour, of discovering the mystery and exciting uniqueness of another person. It's important at all ages; without it life can be lonely, empty, isolated. It's the best gift we can give one to another.

>   To trust a friend and be trusted is one of life's fullest experiences.
>   It is something we need at the depths of our being –
>   to know we can be open with another and not be let down.
>   Trusting means letting go of some part of yourself and not losing it;
>   it's like a mother giving a smile or a friend sharing a secret.
>   Neither is the poorer for it.
>   Trust grows only where there is willingness
>   to share yourself rather than your possessions,
>   and rejoice in the mystery that we are not all the same
>   but that each person is a unique creation and word of God.
>   Each time we trust we share in the life of God,
>   who is faithful always, trustworthy through this life
>   and into an eternity of joy and love.
>   (*Masses with Young People*, D. Neary, pp. 23, 35)

135 But how do you make friends? Many people, specially young people, ask themselves this question and become miserable, locked in the prison of the self, because they don't think they are popular. Yet they are like prisoners with keys in their hands! For we make friends by being friendly. On the whole, people think about us precisely as we think about them. If we dislike them, they adopt the same attitude. If deep down we can't be bothered with them, they won't cross the street to meet us. It is only when we give that we receive. It is those who give love who get it back.

   If you ask 'how can I make myself more attractive?' you ought to notice that the really attractive person is usually the one who takes a real interest in other people. If you ask 'what's the answer to all my problems?' you probably need to go out and get to know someone with far greater problems, who will teach you what courage and happiness mean – and will richly repay any friendship you can offer.
           (*What Anglicans Believe*, D. Edwards, p. 49)

The Christian ideal of friendship

136 Jesus had a group of special friends – the disciples, . . . and he frequently withdrew from the crowd to be with them . . . But he showed an unfailing friendliness to all he met . . .

Those whose hearts were not large enough to understand his universal friendliness misjudged him here, and accused him of being a friend of publicans, mercenary traitors, and sinners. What they saw as shameful the Christian sees as an ideal, beyond his power to realize, but towards which he is turned as he is filled by the spirit of Christ. For this quality, Christians use the word love, by which they mean, not feeling or sentiment, but the resolve to take another person seriously, to understand his feelings and desires and needs and to respond to them, to meet him and to share his life: an unshakable acceptance of responsibility for another person. This is not natural or easy for us beyond the small circle of our familiar friends, but we learn it as we become aware of the 'friendship of Jesus' and discover in his awareness of the Fatherhood of God a sense of the brotherhood of all men.

(*Teenage Religion*, H. Loukes, pp. 117–18)

137 Jesus himself wanted to communicate to his fellow men his perfect trust in the God who loved him. When God began to rule supreme, when his 'kingdom' became reality, love was to be the sphere of human relationships. Being 'converted' meant reacting to this now. Men were to live in an awareness that God loved them, that he had drawn a line under their past and had opened up a new future for them. It also meant that they were to treat their neighbours in the same way, always being concerned for others, keeping faith with them and not rejecting them, and always being ready to forgive, 'seventy times seven'. That meant the end of all attempts at self-assertion, complete detachment from one's possessions, including one's achievements and one's status. When Jesus' disciples told him that he was asking for the moon, that people would never give up what they had, he simply replied, 'For God nothing is impossible.'

(*Jesus*, L Grollenberg, p. 106)

We are 'people who need people'

138 Lord, there are moments, long moments.
when it seems attractive,
living to myself, alone.
Days when people make demands on me,
my time, my energy, emotions.
Times when everyone else is wrong,
and I long to disappear into my dark shell,
a hermit crab, only my claws showing.
Ready to snap at first contact.

Yet if I did, how poor I'd be.
Because rejecting their demands, I reject them.
Leave gaps in my life.
And only when the gaps are narrowed
can the spark of love flash, dance across,
warming my life with light and energy.

Lord, make me sensitive to other people's needs.
Happier to build bridges, sustain relationships.
Help me acknowledge that we're not machines . . .
But people who need people,
and the loving kindnesses that make life good.

(*No Strange Land*, E. Askew, p. 75)

139 We live in a world where 'busy' people are equated with successful people. Busyness is a myth – it means hiding behind a façade of feverish activity and not having the time honestly to face one's life and look where it's going. If we look at the great people of the world, they have always got time for others, always time to listen, to treat you as important and valuable. Mother Teresa of Calcutta is in demand all over the world to lecture and talk and run her many convents, homes for the dying and services to the destitute. Yet she is always found among the least important and the unwanted. She will sit and talk with them for she has time, simply because she is really busy. Truly active people do not need to perpetuate the illusion of being busy; their lives are filled with what ultimately counts – other people.

(*All Shall Be Well*, M. Meegan, p. 42)

Getting and having are no substitutes for being loved

140 As you know, I come to the Netherlands only occasionally and so changes strike me more forcibly than if I were living there all the time. I have noticed one thing in particular: increasing prosperity has not made people more friendly toward one another. They're better off; but that new-found wealth has not resulted in a new sense of community. I get the impression that people are more preoccupied with themselves and have less time for one another than when they didn't possess so much. There's more competitiveness, more envy, more unrest and more anxiety. There's less opportunity to relax, to get together informally, and enjoy the little things in life. Success has isolated a lot of people and made them lonely. It seems sometimes as though meetings between people generally happen on the way to something or someone else.

There's always something else more important, more pressing, of more consequence. The ordinary, simple, little, homely things have to make way for something you really ought to be doing: that film you really should see, that country you simply must visit, and this or that event which you've got to attend. And the higher up you get on the ladder of prosperity, the harder it becomes to be together, to sing together, to pray together and to celebrate life together in a spirit of thanksgiving.

Is it so astonishing, then, that in the Netherlands as in other prosperous countries there are so many people who are lonely, depressed and anxious, and are never genuinely happy? At times, I get the feeling that, under the blanket of success, a lot of people fall asleep in tears. And the question that perhaps lies hidden most deeply in many hearts is the question of love. 'Who really cares about me? Not about my money, my contacts, my reputation or my popularity, but just me? Where do I really feel at home, secure, and cherished? Where can I freely say and think what I like without the fear of losing out on love? Where am I really safe? Where are the people with whom I can simply be, without having to worry about the impression I make on them?'

(*Letters to Marc*, H. Nouwen, pp. 37–8)

141 I want to suggest a new Beatitude: 'Blessed are the sincere who pay compliments.'

For I have just had a compliment, and it has changed my day.

I was irritated. Tired. Discouraged. Nothing seemed much use. Now suddenly all this is changed.

I feel a spurt of enthusiasm, of energy and joy. I am filled with hope. I like the whole world better, and myself . . .

Thank you, God, for this simple miracle so available to all of us. And that we don't have to be saints to employ its power.

Remind me to use it more often to heal and lift and fortify other lives: a compliment!

(*I've got to Talk to Somebody, God*, M. Holmes, p. 72)

142 Lord – you have a minute? – this is
   about saying it; putting it into words.
People don't, Lord. Not about the one
   thing they should.
About liking someone.
We don't *say* it, Lord; hardly ever.

Once, Lord, I was talking to a very
   powerful rich tycoon sort of man
   who was inclined to walk a bit by
   himself, like me, and as I left him
   I told him, truthfully, that I liked him.
'I like you,' I said. And suddenly his
   eyes were wet.
It was a surprise; a shock; a disturbance.
Oh, a person needs telling, Lord.
It warms a person, Lord.
A person needs to hear it, Lord,
To teach him how to say it.
A loving contagion of words, a sort of measles.
You catch it, and give it to others.
   Begin the infection, Lord,
   and let it grow to epidemic.

(*You have a minute, Lord?* D. Kossoff, pp. 56–7)

143 We need to feel more – to understand others.
We need to love more – to be loved back.
We need to cry more – to cleanse ourselves.
We need to laugh more – to enjoy ourselves.
We need to see more – other than our own little fantasies.
We need to hear more – and listen to the needs of others.
We need to give more – and take less.
We need to share more – and realize that we are not so different from one another.
We need to create a world where everyone can peacefully live the life they choose.

(S. Polis Schutz, *The Secondary Assembly Book*, ed. T. Jasper, p. 81)

The love of God in action

144 A colleague has recently described to me an occasion when a West Indian woman in a London flat was told of her husband's death in a street accident. The shock of grief stunned her like a blow, she sank into a corner of the sofa and sat there rigid and unhearing. For a long time her terrible tranced look continued to embarrass the family, friends and officials who came and went. Then the schoolteacher of one of her children . . . called and, seeing how things were, went and sat beside her. Without a word she threw an arm around the tight shoulders, clasping them with her full strength. The white check was thrust hard against the brown. Then as the unrelenting pain seeped through to her the newcomer's tears began to flow, falling on their two hands linked in the woman's lap. For a long time that is all that was happening. And then at last the West Indian woman started to sob . . .

That is the embrace of God, his kiss of life . . . And the Holy Spirit is the force in the straining muscles of an arm, the film of sweat between pressed cheeks, the mingled wetness on the backs of clasped hands. He is as close and as unobtrusive as that, and as irresistibly strong.

(*The Go-Between God*, J. Taylor, p. 243)

The Beatitudes (Matthew 5:3–10)

145 *Happy are those who know they are spiritually poor*
— who are aware that they don't have ready answers to the big questions and are prepared to keep looking.

Happy are those who mourn
— who know that there are millions who are suffering physical or social deprivation and who ensure policies are framed primarily to benefit them.

Happy are those who are humble
— who don't see themselves as superior to others but give each person and each people an equal standing.

Happy are those whose greatest desire is to do what God requires
— who are prepared to walk by forgiveness and change their minds and ways; — who look to the longer term and to the interests of all.

Happy are those who are merciful to others
— who don't see others as a market to be exploited but as partners from whom we learn.

Happy are the pure in heart
— who by concentrating on God's larger purposes are freed from the worries and jealousies of immediate quarrels and conflicts.

Happy are those who work for peace
— who make justice and fulfilment for all their steady concern.

Happy are those who are persecuted because they do what God requires
— who are prepared to be awkward and unpopular among their peers and to let their own national interest come off second-best if that can serve the long-term good of all.

(Martin Conway)

PRAYER

146 'It's a complete waste of time if you ask me.'
In a way, you're not far wrong. Prayer has been called 'wasting time with God'. And that's an apt description. It's a bit like people in love. If you asked lovers *why* they spend time together they'd probably say 'Well, we just like being together.' They don't feel the need to be constantly telling each other things, or even talking at all. They like being together just for its own sake. It's the same with prayer. At its heart prayer is a relationship. It's simply wanting to be with God . . .

Another thing people discover when they pray is that the initiative doesn't come from *them*. God isn't waiting for people to pray to him, like someone at the other end of a telephone line. It's the other way round. The initiative comes from *God*. He is present to us all the time. He is to be found in *this* world: in the natural world around us, in other people, and at the deepest centre of *our* being. When anyone prays they are opening themselves to the God who is already there and who continually offers himself to them . . .

People who seriously pray regularly cannot live on a trivial level. In prayer they explore the depth of their lives; they discover more clearly who they are and what their place in the world is. In prayer they open themselves and unite themselves to the Love which is the source of all reality, and learn to share that love with others.

(*How to survive being married to a Catholic*, by R. Gallagher and M. Henesy, pp. 48–9)

147 It is for you to find your own way of praying. One of the wisest things ever said about prayer was this: 'pray as you can, don't pray as you can't.' But it helps to remember also that what is our way of praying at one stage in our lives may not be so satisfactory at the next stage. Our circumstances change, our personalities develop – and so should our prayers. For no one can say before death that he or she has reached the end of the road of prayer. No, when it comes to praying we are all beginners.

(*What Anglicans Believe*, D. Edwards, p. 72)

The human need for prayer

148 Prayer, to the thinking person, is almost inescapable. Even when ... we cry out against God to challenge or deny him, we are praying. Call it nature, instinct, what you will, man is forever driven to try to make contact with the mysterious author of his own being.

We do this not to appease this force or to curry favour for some hoped for life beyond this one. We do this because *we've got to talk to somebody*. Especially in times of disappointment, trouble, despair.

The psalmist did this. Lying on some silent hillside after a bloody battle, or simply tending his flocks, he sang of his enemies and his agonies, his mistakes, his remorse, his shattered dreams; he pleaded desperately for solace and for aid. Sometimes he quarrelled with God, often he rejoiced and exhalted him. And again and again he spoke of his burning thirst to find and know his maker.

Today there are few such silent hillsides. We are crowded in upon one another. We are assaulted on all sides by radio, television, the printed word. We are taught to verbalize from a tender age. We have made almost a fetish of 'communication'.

Yet today there is so little genuine communication. The very push and pressure of living among so many people has driven us deeper inside ourselves. There, despite all the talk that swirls around us, we are locked in a lonely prison. It is a secret and special place, a place for our own protection, yet a place of anxieties and fears, where the loneliness can be intolerable, unless we find God there.

(*I've got to Talk to Somebody, God*, M. Holmes, pp. xiii – xiv)

149 As one who has been engaged in pastoral counseling for many years and has spent many thousands of hours in face-to-face encounter with troubled and confused persons ... I am inclined to think that the benefits of counseling might not be necessary if there were a more adequate prayer life practiced by persons who were trying to find their way in life.

Prayer may well be one of the most important resources available to man for the exploration of the frontiers of his consciousness.

(*Understanding Prayer*, E. Jackson, pp. 183, 39)

No longer alone

150 Prayer is an end to isolation. It is living our daily life with someone. With him who alone can deliver us from solitude. For he is the only one we can find in our own heart, the only one to whom we can tell everything that is in us. He is ever present. Intimately. Prayer makes us aware of his presence, which we might not realise if we did not pay attention.

It is a living presence. The presence of him from whom we receive everything. We depend on him fundamentally. We discover his presence within us as we become aware of our total dependence on him . . .

He who does not pray belongs to himself. He is his own territory. He enjoys his independence. He is responsible for himself and he tries to reach his goal by his own efforts. He who prays knows that he needs another. Gradually he realises how much he needs this other to whom he turns in prayer, how he cannot live without him, how he can belong to none other but him who is his whole life.

(LeFevre in *Courage to Pray*, A. Bloom and G. LeFevre, p. 73–4)

151 In moments of deep distress and disaster where it would be natural to pray, in that sense I can't pray and this is one of the things we athiests must do without. I can see that it could be the greatest of strength and comfort to feel you could address a prayer and this perhaps is why I think people address prayers, but we can't do it.

(M. Laski in *God and Man*, A. Bloom with M. Laski, p. 24)

152 Psychologically we each need someone who will listen to us. Such a human person is not easy to find though deep relationships provide this atmosphere of mutual listening, in love. If you can accept God as 'the One who listens', then talking to him about yourself (and everything and everyone in your life) makes sense. But it also makes sense to learn how you listen to him without just chattering on. This learning is not all that easy, because we need to learn to still ourselves; and we do not listen with the physical ear, but somehow in a way unknown, we become aware of the still small voice which 'speaks' to our stillness . . . the voice of 'the One who listens'. Once you know or experience this, you listen as he listens — and it spreads to everything and continues always all the time, and this is when we can say that silence speaks to silence.

(*The One Who Listens*, M. Hollings and E. Gullick, pp. 19–20)

Prayer helps us to focus our minds on God

153 There is a vastly misleading idea of prayer as a sort of interminable conversation with a friendly psycho-analyst, to whom we tell all our troubles and makes various requests . . .

That whole view of prayer is fundamentally mistaken God is not anxiously hovering around, waiting to hear what we are going to ask for or to find out who is ill in the neighbourhood. He is not constantly deciding which prayers to answer and which to throw out. He is not interested in the slightest in being praised for being such a good chap or thanked for being such a generous one.

The fundamental point of prayer is that we are trying to direct our minds to focus on the reality of God, to allow ourselves to be filled with a greater realization of his presence, and to be guided in our own actions by the presence of his demand for goodness and love. Prayer is the practice of the realization of God in our own lives.

(*The Living God*, K. Ward, p. 79)

154 Prayer is principally the means by which we maintain a right relationship to God. It is not as so many people think, a means of persuading God to act in their lives and in the world. For people who adopt this attitude, it will not be long before they are thinking of God as a power to be used. These sort of people live not in the world of the Christian Faith but in the world of magic. If we want something done in a certain situation we ought, in faith, to do something about it. If man will not end war, though we pray for ever, God will not end it for man. When we pray for the peace of the world we do not pray in order to inform God about the Middle East, Northern Ireland, etc., nor to give Him information about our anxieties. He knows both better than we. Nor do we pray in order to persuade Him to take the agony of human freedom and responsibility from us and intervene, to alter them. We pray in order to express our compassion for humanity and our anxiety about its present and future, together with our continuing trust in God. We hold together in the presence of God the situation that saddens us. We do this because this is the way Christian love functions. We do it because we believe this relationship of trust is what God desires. When we pray in faith to God this means we are prepared for things to go either way. For the Christian believes that all of us, whether we live or die, belong to God.

(D. Sweetman in *The Trident*, Oct. 1987, pp. 3–4)

155 What happens to self-pity when a person prays with the real joy of thanksgiving? Perspective is changed, blessings appear where least expected, and life becomes a thing of joy and wonder.

What happens when the self-willed person bows in confession? He sees himself as he is. He measures himself by a will beyond his own. He sees the weakness of his ways and returns to the disciplined life that is subject to a higher will . . .

What happens when the person steeped in self-condemnation finds the satisfaction of God's redeeming and forgiving love made real to him? He no longer finds satisfaction in guilt feelings or self-condemnation, but rises above it in joy and appreciation of the restoration of his self-regard.

(*Understanding Prayer*, E. Jackson, pp. 168–69)

Asking-prayers

156 I never pray with greater intensity than when I think I am going to miss a train — a form of suffering which occurs to me frequently.

There seem to be two schools of thought about petitionary prayer. One, which is a sub-department of the 'We are all little children before our heavenly Father and should behave as such' group, is all for even the silliest petitions. The other cautions a certain discretion in what we ask for — partly, perhaps, for the very good reason that petitionary prayer has a high failure rate. (I have noticed, for instance, that I never do catch the trains that I pray to catch; and it would, in fact, take a miracle to get me aboard them, since I never start on time.) . . .

On the other hand, I doubt whether I shall ever stop praying to catch trains which I am, inevitably, going to miss; and it occurs to me that, when I do so, I am giving voice to a much greater distress than that of missed appointments and irritated friends. I am perhaps expressing the fundamental quarrel each of us has with God — why did I have to be *this* kind of a person, caught for ever in the same exasperating set of personality patterns? . . .

The person who has taught me most about petitionary prayer was a man who did not think he had any religious belief at all.

Did he ever pray? I asked him once — curious as to how anyone could get by, particularly as a traveller on British Rail, without constant commerce with God. No, he never prayed to catch trains. Did he pray when he was ill? No, he had been rushed off to hospital not long before with a dangerous illness, but it had not occurred to him to pray. Did he pray for people he loved? No, he didn't pray for people he loved.

One thing, though, he said, after thinking it over, though you couldn't really call it prayer, was that, when he was up against it, in some way he found himself asking for strength just to carry on. Asking? Asking whom? He didn't know whom; he just asked.

(*Christian Uncertainties*, M. Furlong, pp. 83–5)

Prayer moves us beyond the superficialities of life

157 In contemporary society our Adversary majors in three things: noise, hurry, and crowds. If he can keep us engaged in 'muchness' and 'manyness', he will rest satisfied. Psychiatrist C. G. Jung once remarked, 'Hurry is not *of* the Devil; it *is* the Devil.'
If we hope to move beyond the superficialities of our culture – including our religious culture – we must be willing to go down into the recreating silences, into the inner world of contemplation. In their writings, all of the masters of meditation strive to awaken us to the fact that the universe is much larger than we know, that there are vast unexplored inner regions that are just as real as the physical world we know so well. They tell us of exciting possibilities for new life and freedom. They call us to the adventure, to be pioneers in this frontier of the Spirit. Though it may sound strange to modern ears, we should without shame enroll as apprentices in the school of contemplative prayer.

(*Celebration of Discipline*, R. Foster, p. 13)

158 Prayer is the search for God, encounter with God, and going beyond this encounter in communion ... It arises from the awareness that the world in which we live is not simply two dimensional, imprisoned in the categories of time and space, a flat world in which we meet only the surface of things, an opaque surface covering emptiness. Prayer is born of the discovery that the world has depths; that we are not only surrounded by visible things but that we are also immersed in and penetrated by invisible things. And this invisible world is both the presence of God, the supreme, sublime reality, and our own deepest truth. Visible and invisible are not in opposition ... They are present simultaneously, as fire is present in red hot iron ... Living only in the visible world is living on the surface; it ignores or sets aside not only the existence of God but the depths of created being. It is condemning ourselves to perceiving only the world's surface.

(A. Bloom in *Courage to Pray*, A. Bloom and G. LeFevre, pp. 5–6)

'When I try to "pray" deliberately, it is gone'

159 The more I struggle with the idea of prayer, the more I discover that what I am really after is a deepened awareness. Awareness of what? The pat answer is, of course, God; but, if I only succeeded in becoming more aware of the natural world of other people, of the world of movement within my own body, I should feel that I had come to know more about God.

How is this awareness attained? It is here, I think, that one of the great divides between different groups of Christians occurs . . .

One group conceives of prayer as a regular discipline, a daily or nightly exercise . . .

The other group claims to find this 'discipline' of prayer an impossibility; members of it may refuse to use prayers that need words, and to prefer 'sitting' in silence. They would claim that their whole life is their prayer . . .

We know little as yet about the psychology of prayer, but what I suspect we may be dealing with is people who attain awareness through a concentration, a 'sharpening' of their faculties and those who do so through relaxing concentration, through a 'diffusing' of their faculties.

The first group do best by fixing their minds in a particular way, the second by letting their minds run free. Since I come squarely in the second group, I know that for me prayer is, as it were, something seen out of the corner of the eye. When I am writing, or reading, or cooking, or watching television, or talking to friends and family, I am slipping in and out of the awareness that is precious to me. When I try to 'pray' deliberately, it is gone.

(*Christian Uncertainties*, M. Furlong, pp. 78–9)

160 For a prayer need not be a rhetorical address, or an itemized petition, or lips moved soundlessly inside a cathedral, or even words spoken into the air. A prayer may be a wordless inner longing, a sudden outpouring of love, a yearning within the soul to be for a moment united with the infinite and the good, a humbleness that needs no abasement or speech to express, a cry in the darkness for help when all seems lost, a song, a poem, a kind deed, a reaching for beauty, or the strong, quiet inner reaffirmation of faith.

A prayer in fact can be anything that is created of God that turns to God.   (*Ludmila*, P. Gallico, p. oo)

Prayer in everyday life

161 Half guiltily, I realized that the only times I really felt in contact with what I sought, and drew help and encouragement from it, were those spontaneous times when prayers simply leaped up of their own volition, in words, in songs, sometimes even in such acts as dancing, swimming, or scrubbing a floor.

A sense of being able to talk to somebody, or of expressing adulation and gratefulness through ordinary, everyday acts. And a growing conviction that while it is good and right to go to a formal place of worship, it is even more important to worship God wherever we are. All altars are not confined to churches. Your altar may be your desk, the machine you operate, the kitchen stove. The Lord of Life may be known and adored through any deed that we dedicate to him and to the benefit of other people, whether that deed be typing a letter, turning out shoes, or making a family's dinner.

I learned that simply to ask a blessing upon one's circumstances, whatever they are, is somehow to improve them, and to tap some mysterious source of energy and joy.

(*I've got to Talk to Somebody, God*, M. Holmes, pp. xv, xiv)

162 A certain lay reader was once trying to explain to a group of children what paying attention to God in prayer meant, and he related the story of a lady in church who was exhibiting signs of restiveness during worship and at last got up and went out. Afterwards she explained to the lay reader that she had left something cooking and forgotten about it, and during the whole service she had been thinking of this and at last felt she must go home. The lay reader explained this as lack of attention to God. In discussion afterwards Mary, aged 12, said, 'perhaps God was telling her that if she didn't go home the meal would be spoilt and there might be a fire, which would be bad for her family and her home. Perhaps she was listening to God rather than to you conducting the service.' That girl was already vocalizing an approach to prayer which understood its relevance to daily living in a way that the lay reader did not.

(*Prayer in the Secular City*, D. Rhymes. pp. 90–91)

Prayer as a way of life

163 Prayer is not a part-time occupation for any of Christ's disciples – nor indeed is it so for any truly religious man. . . .

To live in constant prayer, to lead a contemplative life, is nothing else than to live in the actual presence of God . . .
God is always present to us. There is no time and no place in our daily life or occupations in which God is not present to us; there are not even certain times or occupations in which God is more present to us or less present to us. God is always the same, the Almighty, the Infinite, the Eternal. He does not change, neither does he 'come' or 'go' from one place to another. Everywhere and always he is, he is himself in his fulness; there is no sense in which he can be more 'here' or less 'there', since he is indivisible. . . .

The life of prayer, the life of contemplation, is simply to realize God's Presence to us. It is therefore not a special way of life reserved for those few individuals who are called to get away from the world and to dwell in the deserts. Contemplation and prayer ought to be the very breath of every disciple of Christ. . . .

To live in the presence of God should be as natural for a Christian as to breathe the air which surrounds him. . . . Do we say: 'Let us first think of the air which surrounds us and then breath?' Willingly, unwillingly, consciously, unconsciously, we breathe and go on breathing; continuously, too, air is entering our lungs. So it is also with the divine Presence which is more essential to our life, to our very being, than the air which we breathe.

(*Prayer*, Abhishiktananda, pp. 1–3, 2, 5)

164 Lord of my days
I have so often said, 'Teach me to pray'. . . .
But there are times when words fail me,
When all the prayers I've ever heard or read
Seem inappropriate,
And the jumble of thoughts,
Worries, questions,
Rushing through my head
Reduce me to silence,
Or the single plea,
'Lord, help me.'

Time has taught me
That I can pray without words.
You, who number the hairs on my head,
Know my every thought.

You know the decisions I must make,
Every problem, every failure,
Every triumph, every joy
Is known to you.
And it is enough to close my eyes,
To come into your presence and say,
'Lord, you know what is happening to me,
In my work, in my marriage,
In my mind and in my body.
Loving Lord, help me.'

And now at last I dimly see
That prayer is not only words
But a way of living,
An awareness of your presence,
A perception of the power of your Spirit in my life;
Supporting me,
Healing me,
Loving me.
Lord
Teach me to pray
With my life.

(*Lord of my days*, F. Topping, pp. 5–7)

165   The communication between myself and God is basic, like the communication between the foetus and the womb that contains it.

The foetus is me. The womb is the whole universe in its living fruitfulness and in the dynamic of evolution which is history.

I feel myself watched by God through the light that surrounds me and the stars that are above me; I feel myself touched by Him in the wind that reaches me, the water that wets me, the hunger that stimulates me, the matter that collides with me and wounds me.

I feel that He begets me through the crock full of bread, the friend who talks to me, the grief that makes me cry, the joy that delights me.

I am never outside of Him, far from Him, without Him.

If praying means 'being in God', then I can say that I pray everywhere because everywhere is His temple.

To say, 'I can't pray because I've got work to do' is absurd.

Who is stopping you from praying while you work? Isn't it better to believe that while working you can be at prayer?

Why reduce prayer to word, thought, place, time?

Go beyond all that.

If by prayer you understand communicating with a Presence, and if this Presence is everywhere, then you can always be at prayer.

If only to communicate.

And to communicate means to love.

It is in loving that you pray, because it is love that carries you to the loved person, and you can love through talking, crying, thinking, walking, sleeping, always, always, always. Twenty-four hours out of twenty-four.

(*The Desert in the City*, C. Carretto, pp. 32–3)

Contemplation

166 One of the first things to understand is the importance of sitting and doing nothing in front of God . . .

Learn to remain in interior respose, peacefully and tranquilly, in spite of the telephone, in spite of someone's knocking at the door, in spite of the demon's saying to you: 'And you have forgotten this . . . .; you still have to get this done by such-and-such an hour . . .

If you learn to stop time, to manage it in this way one, two, three, ten times a day, for longer and longer moments, you will come to the time when you can do it at any time, no matter what your activity, no matter what the word or thought, whether in the liturgy or in everyday life . . . Thus you will be able to be interior to yourself, constantly face to face with God, asking Him unceasingly what you must do, what you must listen to.

(*God and Man*, A. Bloom, pp. 105, 106)

167 Contemplation involves looking to God himself; gazing upon him and delighting in him for his own sake. This can be a richer form of prayer than meditation, as being with a person and enjoying them is more satisfying than simply thinking about them.

(*Prayer and the Pursuit of Happiness*, R. Harries, p. 27)

168 Man is made not merely to work with his hands and to think with his mind, but also to *adore* in the deep silence of his heart. Even more than to adore he is called to plunge into that silence and to lose himself there, unable to utter any word, not even a word of adoration or of praise; for no word can express the mystery of God, the mystery of man in the presence of God . . . There the mind cannot even think or conceive a thought, for it is over-whelmed, silenced, blinded by this light.

(*Prayer*, Abhishiktananda, pp. 28–9)

William Barclay, a twentieth-century Christian writer, draws together some points about prayer.

169   Because I believe in God and in the love of God, I believe in prayer. But over the years of life I have learned certain things about prayer, things which it is essential to remember. I think that there are a great many people who do not pray because they have come to the conclusion that prayer just does not 'work', and that therefore there is no point in prayer.

First, I believe that God will not do for me what I can do for myself. Prayer must never be regarded as a labour-saving device. If I am ill, if there is something wrong with my body, I need not pray for cure, unless I am prepared to take my trouble to the physician, unless I am prepared to sacrifice certain habits and pleasures, unless I am prepared to accept a certain discipline in my life. But if I do patiently and strictly and obediently carry out the regimen that is prescribed for me, then I can pray, and the prayer will put me into a condition in which the treatment will be doubly effective.

Second, I do not think that it is right to pray for things. The one thing to be said about this is that it is an acid test of a thing if you can talk about it and mention it and think about it in the presence of God at all. But I cannot think that it is right to pray for a new house or a new car or a new typewriter or even a new job. I may pray to make the best possible use of what I have, and to do the best possible work where I am; but it is not the part of prayer to ask for material things. Jesus refused to use his power to turn the stones into bread.

Third – and this I think is the most important lesson that the years have taught me – I do not think that prayer is ever evasion, that prayer saves us from having to face things which we do not want to face, and which are going to hurt if we face them. Jesus in Gethsemane discovered that there was no evasion of the Cross. . . . What prayer does is to enable us, not to find a way round the hard thing, but to go straight through it, not to avoid it but to accept it and overcome it. Prayer is not evasion; prayer is conquest. Prayer does not offer me a way of escape; it offers me a way to victory. Jesus did not evade the Cross; he went through the Cross to the

Resurrection. . . . So I must not pray: 'Lord, take this from me.' I must pray: 'Lord, help me to face this thing and to conquer it, and even out of the tragedy to find the glory.'

Fourth, I believe that real prayer is simply being in the presence of God. When I am in trouble, and when I go to my friend, I don't want anything from him except himself, I just want to be with him for a time, to feel his comradeship, his concern, his caring round me and about me, and then to go out to a world warmer because I spent an hour with him. It must be that way with me and God. I must go to him simply for himself. And that is why I believe in intercessory prayer. I don't know the rationale of intercessory prayer. I know that God knows far better than I do what my loved ones need. I know that he does not need to be reminded of their need. But I also know what it has meant to me in the hard times of life to know that there were those who were remembering me before God. I don't know how prayer works – but then I don't know how electricity works either. I do not need to know how a thing works in order to use it and to depend upon it.

(*Testament of Faith*, W. Barclay, pp. 46–8)

Prayer is . . .

170 There are other types of prayer, almost as varied as human experience itself. There is the prayer of finding God in his beauty, in music, in dance, in interpersonal relationships. There is the prayer of meditation, the prayer of silence. But the kind of prayer in which God is my conversational partner, the prayer of mutual self-disclosure is the staple of my own prayer life. I find and worship him in nature, in music and poetry, in my brothers and sisters, in the lightning and thunder over my Sinais and in the burning bushes of Chicago. But I have a feeling that, if I did not come to know him in this prayer of conversation, I would not be attentive to his presence in these other places, especially in the soft, still whispers of the currents of grace that move almost imperceptibly around me.

(He Touched Me, J. Powell, p. 83)

171 Prayer is not a dirgeful, monotonous activity, it is a passionate and dynamic movement of the depths of my being. It is the stirring of everything good in me and the caress of his hand as we grow in his light. Prayer is ultimately the only way forward to a better world since it is the door by which we become our better selves, it is the movement to the eternal in our little hearts, the dawn of the most sacred, dwelling in our fragile mortal beings. . . .

Prayer is the resurrection of God in you, the dawning of happiness. It is a cry in the dark, a burst of light, a glimmer of something unseen, a knowing of what is forever unknowable. The language of prayer is God himself moving in us, in our minds, our desires and actions and making them channels of his peace.

(All Shall Be Well, M. Meegan, pp. 94, 95)

PEACE

Peace begins with me

172 Our earth is stained in blood, divided by hatred and blinded by greed; it is a world worried about tomorrow, uncertain of today, and guilty of yesterday. It is an earth unsatisfied and frightened of itself . . .

While looking upon the strife and violence of the world at large, we sometimes bow our heads in shame at how much men seen to hate each other and that more than half of the global budget is dedicated to weapons, armies and military spending.

   When we look into ourselves, we see that we too pour a lot of energy and resources into self-protection and defence, in more subtle ways. The answer can only be a personal one, it can only be driven by my own commitment. The coming together of humanity begins with me and you, our overcoming of fear and scepticism, our walking through life in the spirit of St Francis, being channels of peace, instruments of kindness and generosity. Unity comes from the daily, hourly response to loving each other.

(All Shall Be Well, M. Meegan, pp. 18, 114)

173 Lord Christ, sometimes we are strangers on this earth, disconcerted by all the violence, the harsh oppositions.

   Like a gentle breeze, you breathe upon us the Spirit of peace.

   Transfigure the deserts of our doubts and prepare us to be bearers of reconciliation wherever you place us, until a hope of peace arises in the world.

(Brother Roger in *Meditations on The Way of the Cross*, Mother Teresa and Brother Roger, p. 43)

Help us to see the best in people

174 There is something lovable in every one. One surprising testimony to this is at funerals. People almost invariably try to find something nice to say about the departed. They may have disliked, despised or hated their guts when they were alive. Yet few are prepared to say 'Thank God he (or she) has gone!' They try to find *something* about the dead person which they can affirm. If we can do this when a person is dead, there is no reason why we cannot do it before they die. There is, as a matter of fact, something lovable about every person, for they only exist because God loves them. Our task is to see: to see what Gods sees; to see in them what God sees in them; what is truly in them because God created them.

(Prayer and the Pursuit of Happiness, R. Harries, p. 144)

175 We hold in your presence, O Lord,
all those we love and those who love us.
Your love is so much greater than ours
and you work unceasingly for our well-being,
With all the resources of infinite wisdom and patience.
Bestow on them the fullness of your blessing.

Heavenly Father,
give me a genuine love for others,
both those I like and those I don't like;
help me to overcome my fears and prejudices
and to see your image in all men.

O Christ who welcomed the downtrodden,
those made to feel small,
help us to enlarge others rather than diminish them;
to build up rather than to belittle.

(Prayer and the Pursuit of Happiness, R. Harries, p. 152)

Trying to love our enemies

176 In relationships there are some people whom we instinctively like. There seems to be a pre-ordained harmony between us, and we flourish in each other's company ... It is not difficult to flow out from our depth to such people. Towards others we feel neutral, some we tolerate in polite silence, and a few we find unbearable. And yet we have to love them all without in any way demanding that they change their character to conform with our own wishes. We have to learn that love is not an emotional response or a feeling. It is a state of willed tranquillity in which we can absorb the personality of the other individual and give of our very being to him. Indeed, we can do none of this on our own, but depend on the Holy Spirit to lighten our soul with love.

(*Summons to Life*, M. Israel, p. 43)

177 Nothing harder is ever asked of any of us than to love our enemies; in fact it is so difficult that some of us cannot achieve it at all.

It is possible to cheat by not choosing to notice the feelings of anger, revenge, and violence others evoke in us – I have done it on and off for years. We can then appear in our own eyes as loving people; only we usually give the game away by the unkind things we say – either to people's faces or behind their backs, it scarcely matters which. If we are clever people we do it cleverly, and probably amusingly. If we are less clever we do it clumsily. But it causes pain. Hatred has as much necessity to find expression as the mosquito has to sting.

The first step towards loving one's enemies is not the suppression of hateful feelings ... but the courageous discovery of them. ...

It is painful to discover violent feeling within. Sometimes it seems helpful to acknowledge our anger to our adversary. 'I did hate you when you said ...' often seems to clear the air remarkably, particularly in the closest relationships – not least because the admission nearly always gives useful information. We often do not know when we are arousing anger in others, and they are similarly blind about us.

(*Christian Uncertainties*, M. Furlong, pp. 24–5)

Martin Luther King explains why we should love our enemies

178 *Why should we love our enemies?* The first reason is fairly obvious. Returning hate for hate multiplies hate, adding deeper darkness to a night already devoid of stars. Darkness cannot drive out darkness — only light can do that. Hate cannot drive out hate, only love can do that. Hate multiplies hate, violence multiplies violence and toughness multiplies toughness in a descending spiral of destruction. So when Jesus says 'Love your enemies,' he is setting forth a profound and ultimately inescapable admonition. Have we not come to such an impasse in the modern world that we must love our enemies — or else? The chain reaction of evil — hate begetting hate, wars producing more wars — must be broken, or we shall be plunged into the dark abyss of annihilation. . . . Love is the only force capable of transforming an enemy into a friend. We never get rid of an enemy by meeting hate with hate; we get rid of an enemy by getting rid of enmity. By its very nature, hate destroys and tears down; by its very nature, love creates and builds up. Love transforms with redemptive power . . .

Of course, this is not *practical*. Life is a matter of getting even, of hitting back, of dog eat dog. . . .

My friends, we have followed the so-called practical way for too long a time now, and it has led inexorably to deeper confusion and chaos. Time is cluttered with the wreckage of communities which surrendered to hatred and violence. For the salvation of our nation and the salvation of mankind, we must follow another way. This does not mean that we abandon our righteous efforts. With every ounce of our energy we must continue to rid this nation of the incubus of segregation. But we shall not in the process relinquish our privilege and our obligation to love. Whilst abhorring segregation, we shall love the segregationist. This is the only way to create the beloved community.

To our most bitter opponents we say: 'We shall match your capacity to inflict suffering by our capacity to endure suffering. We shall meet your physical force with soul force. Do to us what you will, and we shall continue to love you. We cannot in all good conscience obey your unjust laws, because non-co-operation with evil is as much a moral obligation as is co-operation with good. Throw us in jail, and we shall still love you. Send your hooded perpetrators of violence into our community at the midnight hour and beat us and leave us half dead, and we shall still love you. But be ye assured that we will wear you down by our capacity to suffer. One day we shall win freedom, but not only for ourselves. We shall so appeal to your heart and conscience that we shall win *you* in the process, and our victory will be a double victory.'

Love is the most durable power in the world. This creative force, so beautifully exemplified in the life of our Christ, is the most potent instrument available in mankind's quest for peace and security.

I would not wish to give the impression that nonviolence will accomplish miracles overnight. Men are not easily moved from their mental ruts or purged of their prejudiced and irrational feelings. When the underprivileged demand freedom, the privileged at first react with bitterness and resistance. Even when the demands are couched in nonviolent terms, the initial response is substantially the same . . . But the nonviolent approach does something to the hearts and souls of those committed to it. It gives them new self-respect. It calls up resources of strength and courage that they did not know they had. Finally, it so stirs the conscience of the opponent that reconciliation becomes a reality.

(*Strength to Love*, M. L. King, pp. 51, 52, 54–55, 152)

Forgiveness

179 Let us be practical and ask the question, *How do we love our enemies?*

First, we must develop and maintain the capacity to forgive. He who is devoid of the power to forgive is devoid of the power to love. It is impossible even to begin the act of loving one's enemies without the prior acceptance of the necessity, over and over again, of forgiving those who inflict evil and injury upon us. . . .

Forgiveness does not mean ignoring what has been done or putting a false label on an evil act. It means, rather, that the evil act no longer remains as a barrier to the relationship. Forgiveness is a catalyst creating the atmosphere necessary for a fresh start and a new beginning. It is the lifting of a burden or the cancelling of a debt. The words 'I will forgive you, but I'll never forget what you've done' never explain the real nature of forgiveness. Certainly one can never forget, if that means erasing it totally from his mind. But when we forgive, we forget in the sense that the evil deed is no longer a mental block impeding a new relationship. Likewise, we can never say, 'I will forgive you, but I won't have anything further to do with you.' Forgiveness means reconciliation, a coming together again. Without this, no man can love his enemies. The degree to which we are able to forgive determines the degree to which we are able to love our enemies.

(*Strength to Love*, M. L. King, pp. 48–9)

180 FATHER, to whom we pray 'forgive us our sins, as we forgive those who sin against us.'
Give us the courage, the love and generosity to forgive others.
That we may have the healing that forgiveness brings,
rather than be constantly picking at old sores;
That we may have the freedom that forgiveness brings,
rather than be imprisoned by memories of those who have hurt us;
And that we may grow to our full stature,
rather than be stunted by feelings of bitterness and resentment.
We ask this, knowing that we also are in need of forgiveness.

Amen

(J. Thompson)

181   Forgiveness is the source and the rock
of those who share their lives:
- to forgive each day,
- to forgive and forgive and forgive,
- and to be forgiven just as many times . . .

Forgiveness is the cement that bonds us together:
it is the source of unity;
it is the quality of love;
that draws togetherness out of separation.
Forgiveness is understanding and holding
the pain of another;
it is compassion.
Forgiveness is the acceptance of our own brokenness,
yours and mine.
Forgiveness is letting go of unrealistic expectations of others
and of the desire that they be other than they are.
Forgiveness is liberating others to be themselves,
not making them feel guilty for what may have been.
Forgiveness is to help people flower, bear fruit,
and discover their own beauty.
Forgiveness does not need the drama of tears
and emotional hugging.
It is a simple gesture,
signifying that we are together, part of the one body,
called by Jesus
in a covenant with one another.
Forgiveness is peace-making:
struggling to create unity,
to build one body,
to heal the broken body of humanity.
Forgiveness is to follow Jesus,
to be like him,
for he came to give and to forgive,

(The Broken Body, J. Vanier, pp. 106–107)

182 The terrible spectre of the mushroom cloud,
of the nuclear bomb,
looms over humanity –
this folly of mankind,
driven in a race for superiority in weapons and warfare.
All the money and human resources being poured
into the manufacture of bombs,
the making of new, more destructive weapons,
weapons that will operate more quickly, more precisely,
more powerfully, more totally –
while many women in Africa still spend hours each day
just bringing water to their homes!

Never before has the cry for peace been so great.
Never before has the danger been so immense.
Today our earth, our beautiful earth,
could be totally shattered,
ruined by these weapons.
Today conflict is too dangerous,
for all life could be destroyed.
With all the vast sophistication in our weaponry
we are at the mercy
of a momentary error
in human judgement or technical functioning.
We know that and are filled with fear.

Yet everywhere armed conflict *is* rampant:
terrorism of all sorts is increasing.
People are imprisoned, tortured or disappear.
Dictatorships, whether marxist or military,
are crushing people,
preventing them from speaking,
taking from them their human rights.
And there is the weak and painful cry
of the unborn child aborted
or of the unwelcome child with disabilities.

And, more and more, those who were crushed or put aside
are rising up in anger and frustration,
in armed revolt
to claim their place, their land, their right to live.
Is violence the only solution?
Is there any other way?
For violence always engenders violence.
How often the ideals of liberation
are swallowed up in
more terrible violence,
more total oppression!
Can there be another way to peace?

(*The Broken Body*, J. Vanier, pp. 7–8)

183 Father, Forgive . . .

The hatred which divides nation from nation,
   race from race, class from class,
Father, forgive.
The covetous desires of people and nations
   to possess what is not their own,
Father, forgive.
The greed which exploits the work of human hands,
   and lays waste the earth,
Father, forgive.
Our envy of the welfare and happiness of others,
Father, forgive.
Our indifference to the plight of the imprisoned,
   homeless, the refugee,
Father, forgive.
The lust which dishonours
   the bodies of men and women,
Father, forgive.
The pride which leads to trust in ourselves
   and not in God,
Father, forgive.

(The Coventry Cathedral Prayer)

184 The secret of faith and love is the sacred art of forgiving. All of us have one thing in common, from bishops to pop stars, pensioners to schoolchildren, rich and poor: we are all weak, we are all frail, and we fall many times each day. None of us are as good as we could be, we could all be better, gentler, more merciful. We all remember moments when we caused another person to be very sad or dejected . . . We all know of the times we could have been generous and weren't. The nature of real love can be summarized in a single word, the art of being human can be summarized in the fullness and breadth of that same word: forgiveness. . . .

What is important is not to find out the sins and weaknesses of each other, but to forgive, to drop it when we have a stone to throw. When someone stands in front of us and we are in the right whilst they are naked and vulnerable, let it go. It is only when we confront the other in their weakness and forgive that real love is born.

(All Shall Be Well, M. Meegan, pp. 57, 52)

185 I had a paint box
but it didn't have the colour red
for the blood of the wounded,
nor white
for the hearts and faces of the dead.

It didn't have yellow either
for the burning sands
of the desert.

Instead it had orange
for the dawn and the sunset
and blue
for new skies
and pink
for the dreams of young people.

I sat down and painted peace.

(Lifelines, p. 6, poem by a child of 10)

Christ's arms outstretched in peace

186 For Christians in South Africa, the cost of working for peace, against the violent structures of apartheid, demands a depth of discipleship we may find hard to imagine . . .

In Johannesburg, Khotso House (the Sesotho name means 'peace'), has been the home of one of Christian Aid's partners, the South African Council of Churches (SACC). Its struggle for real peace in society is powerfully symbolized by a large wall-hanging in the foyer of Khotso House, that shows Christ opening his arms to the sufferings of his people, and it proclaims 'peace' in the six languages used in South Africa. Included in the work of the SACC is arranging legal representation for political detainees, and giving counselling and practical help to their families; encouraging churches to act as places of sanctuary for all whose lives and freedom are in danger from the police and vigilante violence; helping people distinguish, in a time of press censorship, between truth and propaganda in the media; and engaging in theological reflection and witness about the demands of God's kingdom at this critical time.

In August 1988, a blast from the most powerful bomb ever planted in South Africa ripped through Khotso House, causing enormous damage to the building and injuring some maintenance staff. Those who work there are in no doubt that what was being attacked was the determination, to which their Christian discipleship commits them, to see apartheid destroyed. But signs of hope remain. The explosion blew out the main entrance. Now, exposed to view from the street, the great tapestry of peace can be seen undamaged. Christ's arms are still outstretched; but there is also a heap of rubble at his feet. Visiting the building in September, Archbishop Tutu said: 'It seems to say, yes, the powers of evil appear to be on the rampage, but in the end they will not be able to prevail against the force of order, of love, of peace.'

(Christian Aid Publication, Spring 1989, ed. J. Morley)

SUFFERING

'Faith in the City' – the church report of 1986

187 A growing number of people are excluded by poverty or powerlessness from sharing the common life of our nation. A substantial minority – perhaps as many as one person in every four or five across the nation, and a much higher proportion in the urban priority areas – are forced to live on the margins of poverty or below the threshold of an acceptable standard of living.

Another hard-luck story from a developing country? No, this comment is about Britain. It's about the inner cities, home for one third of the population living on three per cent of the country's land.

Put more graphically, one person said: 'We have three problems: poverty, poverty and poverty.'

Of course this is not poverty as it is experienced in parts of the third world. People in Britain are not actually starving. But many people living in the inner cities are deprived, they suffer intolerable housing conditions, poor schooling, the highest unemployment rates, . . . violence and prejudice.

In these conditions frustration has erupted into street violence – as seen in Liverpool, Birmingham, Bristol and London. And in the light of those disturbances, the Archbishop of Canterbury set up a commission in 1983 . . .

As well as the picture of human misery, the commission did find hope, it did find faith in the cities: 'We have observed an amazing variety of human responses to conditions of adversity: we have seen courage, resilience and dedicated service; we have encountered local pride and profound human loyalties. The same is true of the church. Often threatened, often struggling for survival, often alienated from the community it seeks to serve, it is often also intensely alive, proclaiming and witnessing to the gospel more authentically than in many parts of "comfortable Britain".'

(*Network*, U.S.P.G. magazine, July 1986, p. 10)

If God is good and all-power, why is there suffering?

188 The case against the idea that there is a power of love behind the universe is very strong. . . . Droughts, famines, car crashes, murders, cancer, mental illness, senility – all these add up to a formidable case to answer. . . .

First, an obvious point. Much suffering in the world is caused by the negligence, weakness and deliberate wrong doing of human beings. If it is the will of God to create free beings, as opposed to robots or puppets, this is the price he and we have to pay. . . .

If we value being able to make up our own mind and make our own decisions in life then we too have to pay the price of living in a world in which this is possible. We cannot have it both ways. We cannot both be free and have a world in which wrong choices do no damage. This point, if accepted, has wide implications. For much more suffering in the world is attributable to human beings than we sometimes allow. Take the millions of starving. The fact is that there is quite enough food in the world for everyone. But through millions of wrong choices which have brought about the rigid political and economic structures in which we live, there are mountains of surplus food in Europe and America, whilst those in Africa starve to death. Similarly, take the question of earthquakes. The rich can afford to live in earthquake free areas or in reinforced houses. It is the poor who cannot move or protect themselves. It is the poor who suffer.

The second point is that in order to exist as the kind of creatures we are, capable of thinking and choosing, we need a relatively stable environment. I plan my day and make decisions in it on the basis of certain well-founded assumptions, that the sun will come up, that the laws of gravity will operate, that water will boil at a certain temperature and freeze at another one. The consequences of what I do, putting on the electric kettle or putting water in the freezer, are predictable. This means that there is a very strict limit on what God can do in the way of disrupting these scientific laws without frustrating his whole purpose in making the universe in the first place.

(*Evidence for the love of God*, R. Harries, pp. 1–3)

Does God send suffering?

189 There may be a sense in which God is responsible for everything, in that he created the universe. But a sharp distinction has to be made between what God directly wills and what he merely permits as part of his overall purpose. So a parent may be responsible for giving his child permission to drive the family car. But he in no sense wills the subsequent accident that unfortunately occurs. God wills the universe to exist, he lets it be with a life of its own. But he does not will suffering; on the contrary, he opposes it.

(*Evidence for the love of God*, R. Harries, p. 11)

190 One or two people have said to me that God must love and trust me very much to test me with an inoperable cancer. I have never replied to them, partly because I question the theology on which they base their remarks and partly because, if they were right, I frankly wish that God did not trust me so much! I would be quite content with less trust on his part and less suffering on mine. It would be a curious way of showing his love to me, and I cannot imagine that I could even think of inflicting such a thing on my children, had I the power to do so.

A more serious objection to the viewpoint is that numerous people suffer far more acutely than I have ever done, and many of them have clearly been crushed by the test. As a result of their pain they have suffered nervous breakdowns, their marriages have broken up or they have become bitter atheists. If suffering is to be regarded purely as a test of our faith, God at times seems to have miscalculated wildly.

(*Fear No Evil*, D. Watson, pp. 122–123)

Suffering is not an 'act of God'

191 I knew a woman whose daughter was killed by an electrical household accident, electrocuted by an electric blanket. There was a fatal accident enquiry, and the verdict was that it was 'an act of God'. The mother was shattered. Of course, it is only a legal formula to denote something of which the explanation is undiscoverable, but there are few more blasphemous phrases in the English language. At that time there was no one sorrier than God that something which should never have happened had happened to one of his children.

I had in my own experience a wounding attribution of events to the will of God. The BBC asked me to do a week's 'ten to eight' in the morning talks on radio, and they asked me to take as a subject the modern approach to the miracles of Jesus. It was not a subject which I myself would have chosen, but I agreed to do it. The line I took was a line that I have always taken. I have always felt that Jesus is to be regarded, not as a person who *did* things nineteen hundred years ago, but as a person who *does* things now. I therefore said that the miracles were often not so much stories of what Jesus once did, but symbols of what he still can do. I spoke of the stilling of the storm, and I said that if Jesus did still a storm on the Lake of Galilee in AD 28, it meant very little to me. But it is different if the lesson of the story is that in any storm of life there is in the presence of Jesus confidence and calm, that the storms Jesus stills are in the hearts of men, so that, no matter what tempest of trouble or pain or sorrow may blow upon life, with him there is calm.

On the last day of the week instead of a talk I was interviewed by David Winter. He asked me how I had come to this way of looking at things. I told him the truth. I told him that some years ago our twenty-one-year-old daughter and the lad to whom she would some day have been married were both drowned in a yaching accident. I said that God did not stop that accident at sea, But he did still the storm in my own heart, so that somehow my wife and I came through that terrible time still on our own two feet. The letters after the broadcasts began to come in, and there came an anonymous letter from Northern Ireland: 'Dear Dr Barclay, I know now why God killed your daughter; it was to save her from being corrupted by your heresies.' *I know now why God killed your daughter.* That —

the accidental destruction of the beautiful and the good – the will of God. If I had had that writer's address, I would have written back, not in anger – the inevitable blaze of anger was over in a flash – but in pity, and I would have said to him, as John Wesley said to someone: 'Your God is my devil.' The day my daughter was lost at sea there was sorrow in the heart of God.

When things like that happen, there are just three things to be said. First, to understand them is impossible. Second, Jesus does not offer us solutions to them. What he does offer us is his strength and help somehow to accept what we cannot understand. Third, the one fatal reaction is the bitter resentment which for ever after meets life with a chip on the shoulder and a grudge against God. The one saving reaction is simply to go on living, to go on working, and to find in the presence of Jesus Christ the strength and courage to meet life with steady eyes, and to know the comfort that God too is afflicted in my affliction.

(*Testament of Faith*, W. Barclay, pp. 44–6)

Does God stop suffering?

192 It is not right to raise false hopes that prayer will of itself achieve what medical science cannot achieve. Prayer is about attuning yourself to the love of God, who wills all that is good for us, but it does not override the progress of the cancer cell. Thirty years ago, in his Gifford lectures, Professor John Macmurray drew this contrast: The maxim of illusory religion runs: 'Fear not: trust in God and he will see that none of the things you fear will happen to you': that of real religion, on the contrary is: Fear not, the things that you are afraid of are quite likely to happen to you, but they are nothing to be afraid of.'

(*A Year Lost and Found*, M. Mayne, pp. 69–70)

Let's stop asking 'why?'

193 If we have any conception of the greatness of God we should refrain from pressing the question *Why?* however understandable that might be. On many thousands of issues we simply do not and cannot know. Why does God allow the birth of severely handicapped children? I don't know. Why are some individuals plagued with tragedies for much of their lives, whilst others suffer hardly at all? I don't know. Why is there seeming injustice on every side? I don't know. The questions are endless if we ask why? Instead we should ask the question *What?* 'What are you saying to me, God? What are you doing in my life? What response do you want me to make?' With that question we can expect an answer. . . .

More important than anything is knowing God's will and doing it. It is far more important than having intellectual answers to all our philosophical questions about God and man, suffering and pain. Life anyway is short and uncertain, but God's word endures for ever. However, our lives are often so full of other things that we find it impossible to hear or discern what God is saying to us. Our ears are deaf, our minds dull and our wills stubborn. We do not hear God speak, or if we do, we fail to respond.

It is sometimes only through suffering that we begin to listen to God. Our natural pride and self-confidence have been stripped painfully away, and we become aware, perhaps for the first time, of our own personal needs. We may even begin to ask God for help instead of protesting about our condition or insisting on explanations.

(*Fear No Evil*, D. Watson, pp. 129–30)

194 What do you say to people whose lives have been rocked by sudden tragedy? My reaction was that it's a time to listen and help, not to make statements. First, because I have no easy answer to that sort of event. And second, because I don't think people can take in much of what you say, anyway, when their minds are brimming with anxiety and fear. People in shock are not searching for explanations, they are crying out for comfort. That goes beyond reasoned argument, back to a basic need to feel they're not alone. They want to know that someone cares. They need to feel arms round them, something, someone, to ease the pain.

God's love becomes real in these situations, not through sermons, but through quiet listening. They need our time, and maybe our tears, but not our logic. . . .

Lord, if I'm faced with someone's need today,
help me to offer silence.
Not in the coldness of indifference,
but in warm welcome
to hear his version of events.
Help me control the urge to talk,
to people his life with my puppets,
to jump to safe conclusions,
for which I have stock answers.
Teach me, with open mind and heart,
to hear his words and thoughts.
To substitute the clichés I mistake for truth
with quiet love.
Spoken through eyes, not mouth,
in hand, not sermon.
In love, that comes before advice.

(*No Strange Land*, E. Askew, pp. 48–9)

Hopelessness!

195 Now we are approaching the year 2000 –
optimism has given way to hopelessness
and illusions are fading . . .
We can see the pain of our world
as we watch the news,
drinking our beer in the comfort of our sitting room,
with the security of doors locked against any intrusion.
If there is a person in pain in our village
or a house that has burnt down,
or if there is some other local catastrophe,
perhaps we can do something about it.
But what can we do about the things we see on television
happening in the Sahel or in Central America?
What can *we* do to repair the broken body of humanity?
Wars drag on endlessly,
people continue to starve.
Everywhere there are terrible inequalities.
Workers are exploited,
refugees are fleeing in terror.
Peoples are oppressed,
while politicians engage in petty squabbling
and churches fight with one another.
Today, as we approach the year 2000 there appears to be
so little hope.
So perhaps the only thing to do
is to hide in front of our television sets;
and forget the pain of this broken world,
the pain of a broken humanity,
about which we can do nothing.
Let us change the channel when the pictures are too ghastly
and look for other stations,
a tantalizing film,
some other light amusement –
any form of distraction.

(*The Broken Body*, J. Vanier, pp. 4–6)

Hopefulness!

Brave individuals have challenged and changed the face of suffering. They are an inspiration to others.

196   When the young Sue Ryder had first arrived in Poland, she was caught up in the struggles of the Polish people to rebuild their shattered country. The English girl's selfless determination to help galvanised many of those who had been standing on the sidelines.

My friend, Basia, one of Sue's earliest helpers, was one of these. Basia was no stranger to suffering. Her husband, Ryszard, had been arrested and sent to a concentration camp in Germany a few weeks after their marriage; and in the first year of the Occupation her young brother Tadeusz was shot dead in one of the frequent sporadic street round-ups. (When the news of Tadeusz's death was broken to his mother, she burst into tears and said, 'I suppose I must thank God he cannot now be sent to Auschwitz.') When the war was over and Ryszard had returned, Basia had preferred to close her eyes to the misery all around her. 'Before Sue came,' she said, 'there were many of us who knew all about the problems of the chronic sick and their terrible struggle to survive. But there were so *many* problems. In every city and town people were clearing away rubble with their bare hands before rebuilding could start. With so much destruction and misery everywhere we turned, some of us felt paralysed. It was Sue who made the difference. She was full of compassion and afraid of no one. Somehow she showed us what could be done. She opened our eyes, and that was when we found our courage again.'

(Blessings, M. Craig, pp. 107–8)

197   The world is so full of suffering. Unspeakable suffering on the grand scale; desperate lonely suffering in the small events of human life: failures, disappointments, secret agonies.

Help us never knowingly to contribute to that suffering, either by a physical act or a gloating word. Don't let us ever rejoice in another's pain or downfall.

(I've got to Talk to Somebody, God, M. Holmes, p. 79)

We can learn from our suffering

198 I had not been home very long when I received a long letter from an Auschwitz survivor called Stefan. Stefan's wife, who had been in Ravensbrück, had died after the birth of her second child in 1952. Stefan's own health was failing rapidly, and he was trying not to think about the day when he would be forced to stop working. Most Poles in those days took two jobs in order to make ends meet. If Stefan lost his one and only job, he would be in serious trouble.

The letter told me that the blow had fallen. His health had given up. For years he had dreaded this moment, and he knew just how bleak his future prospects were. 'I worry most of all,' said the letter, 'about the children. What will they become?' Having written those words, he must have stopped to reflect on what he had written, for he crossed out the last sentence and wrote: 'No, I must not worry about them. They are in God's hands, and there is only one important thing for them. I hope they will learn to have compassion for others.'

The reflection knocked me sideways, and years later it still does. Suddenly all the accepted ambitions that parents have for their offspring . . . were reduced to size. Health, wealth, reputation, success, fame – where did these stand on any eternal scale of values? Stefan had stumbled on the pearl of great price. . . . In the concentration camps, when all other qualities went to the wall, only loving-kindness had counted. Cleverness, rank, talent were of no account. What kept the spark of humanity alive was compassion – one wounded, stricken human being reaching out to another.

The miracle was that the survivors, in being helped, gave so much in return. They had learned lessons about human values which only those who had lived with death could have learned. They had gained an extra dimension because thay had learned what was important in life and what was not, and because in their daily lives, they were passing on that lesson. Perhaps, in the world's terms, they were abject failures, every one of them – sick, poor, unable to work, with a life that was going nowhere. But as I left Poland, I knew that they were rich beyond measure. And I envied their wholeness, if not the paths by which they had come to it.

(*Blessings*, M. Craig, pp. 109–110, 108)

'Our tragedy is not that we suffer, but that we waste suffering'

199 When (the doctor) had gone, I tried to shut out all thought, because all thoughts led back to the same intolerable one: we now had two mentally handicapped sons, not one. I was screaming inside . . .

The prospect of the long night hours ahead filled me with dread. I didn't see how I could get through them without being destroyed by the fear, anger, panic and shame that were raging inside me. Everything was falling to pieces. The tender shoot of understanding, the fragile hold I had got on the meaning of suffering were swallowed up in the whirlpool in which I was now drowning. Prayer? Not likely. I'd finished with that. I'd tried it, and look where it had got me.

And so the night came on, and I slipped further and further into the abyss. . . .

It was when I had given up hope of ever reaching the bottom, that some words I had once read flashed into my mind with brilliant clarity: 'Our tragedy is not that we suffer, but that we waste suffering. We waste the opportunity of growing into compassion.' The words leaped out at me, acting like a brake on my despair, dramatically halting my slide into madness.

The value of suffering does not lie in the pain of it, which is morally neutral – but in what the sufferer makes of it. Two persons can go through the same painful experience, one be destroyed by it, the other achieve an extra dimension. The real tragedy of suffering is the wasted opportunity.

Next morning, the flowers began to arrive, bringing with them an almost tangible awareness of supportive love and grief. . . .

Congratulations cards were conspicuous by their absence, but in their place came letters. No-one in their right mind could say that they were happy for us, but almost everyone I had ever known, ever only slightly, felt impelled to write, to express deep feelings, or even to apologise for the fact that they did not know how to. One letter which moved me to tears said simply: 'We just don't know what to say, except that you have our love and prayers.' . . .

The letters, representing as they did, so much human feeling, so much anguished groping for words, said more than the spoken word ever could. They could be looked at over and over again, they had a strength out of all proportion to their actual stumbling content, and I still have them all. . . .

I felt I was being upheld by a genuine human response, and it seemed to me the most powerful force in all the world. Those letters did not take the place of prayer, they *were* prayer.

When I finally stopped feeling sorry for myself, I found myself beginning to think deeply about the whole problem of grief and suffering in our lives. More and more I was convinced that, though suffering was itself negative, it could very easily destroy. On the other hand it could be used positively, for growth. It was, in fact, the only means of emotional growth, the route from winter to spring. 'Your pain,' wrote Kahlil Gibran, in 'The Prophet', 'is the breaking of the shell that encloses your understanding. Even as the stone of the fruit must break, that its heart may stand in the sun, so must you know pain.' That seemed to me to reach the heart of the matter. I know that, in my own case, however hard I had been trying to come to terms with the tragedy I had in effect been shutting out the pain, trying to deaden my awareness of it, allowing a rock-hard shell to form and insulate me from it. . . . Building up the shell *was* an answer, but in the end it was a rotten answer; and until that shell could be smashed, there was no hope of personal growth.
Nicky's birth was giving me a second chance, smashing the hard shell with hammer-blows. I was left vulnerable, and when one is vulnerable one has the humility to learn.

(*Blessings*, M. Craig, pp. 64–65, 140, 66–67, 71–72)

200 In *The Wizard of Oz*, Dorothy, the tin man, the cowardly lion and the scarecrow all set off to find the Wizard, the godlike figure who will give them the solution to their problems and change them into what they want to be. When they finally reach the Wizard after many trials and tribulations, they discover that he's just an ordinary man with problems of his own. But they also discover that the very quest for him has effected the sought-after changes in them; they had the answer within themselves all the time. Suffering may be the pressure that calls us to be ourselves. That's not a justification for it and doesn't excuse it, but somehow that same destructive force can be the flame and the anvil which forges us.

(*God for Nothing*, R. Mackenna, p. 163)

201 At the end of the day what really matters is not that we should all get better and live happily ever after, as in some unreal fairy tale. What alone is important is that God's will may be done, and his Kingdom come, in the circumstances of *this* experience, *this* sickness, *this* action . . .

Life is not about fairness or unfairness. It is often unjust, claiming the good and the innocent as its victims. Life is about making certain choices: between one action and another, between generous self-giving and selfish holding back; and it is also about what we make of the harsh, unlooked-for blows that come to us all: sickness and pain, grief and old age. None of us dare judge the life of another: that is God's prerogative, and his judgement is matched by his mercy. Those who become embittered or lose their faith or take their own life in despair may have had the dice loaded against them from the start, and none of us know whether we should have survived if we had been in their place. All I would dare claim is that it is good if we learn from our own experience of suffering or bereavement, and as a result are wiser, more tolerant, above all more compassionate. There are those who are able to use their sickness, their pain, even their dying as a time for growth and a new-found trust in the God who holds us in death as in life and will not let us go. And perhaps they are not as rare as we think.

(*A Year Lost and Found*, M. Mayne, pp. 70–71)

The comfort of God

202 I suppose the essence of being brokenhearted is to be desperately sad about something. Perhaps we've had the sack, so that we haven't got a job to do any more. Perhaps the person whom we love has gone off with someone else . . . and we're feeling hurt and rejected and in a lot of pain. Perhaps we have got an illness that we dread. Or perhaps someone we love has died and there's an aching empty space in our life.

But if we bring the empty space and the heart that is frightened and hurting into the presence of God something seems to happen. I don't know how, but I know it does. There is a comforting and a mending that goes on inside us, and perfect love somehow casts out our fear.

The thing that is hurting us isn't the end of the world. The world is still there, with all the beautiful things that are in it to look at and love – and other people are in it, for us to be friends with and to laugh with and perhaps to cry with.

(*My World*, ed. S. Brown, p. 96, by editor)

Those in need can enrich us

203 Do not neglect your sick and elderly. Do not turn away from the handicapped and the dying. Do not push them to the margins of society. For if you do, you will fail to understand that they represent an important truth. The sick, the elderly, the handicapped and the dying teach us that weakness is a creative part of human living, and that suffering can be embraced with no loss of dignity. Without the presence of these people in your midst, you might be tempted to think of health, strength and power as the only important values to be pursued in life. But the wisdom of Christ and the power of Christ are to be seen in the weakness of those who share in his sufferings. Let us keep the sick and the handicapped at the centre of our lives. Let us treasure them and recognise with gratitude the debt we owe them. We begin by imagining that we are giving to them; we end by realising that they have enriched us.

(*How to survive being married to a Catholic*, R. Gallagher and M. Henesy, p. 11, quoting from Pope John Paul II)

The death of a ten-year old, severely handicapped child.

204 What did we really feel when Paul died – this child of ours who had never ever recognised us? I can only speak for myself, and admit to a confused complexity of emotions. I knew that Paul's death was a release for all of us, and there is no denying that I felt a deep thankfulness that this phase of my life was over. But I felt grief too, most probably for the loss of the child he might have been; and there was the even greater pain of believing that I had failed him. A kind of desolation swamped me for a time, and for nights on end I could do nothing but cry. It was a crying which had no rationale except in remorse, and in some odd way I felt I was not entitled to genuine grief. Our friends were so sure that Paul's death was an unqualified blessing that I felt guilty about the grief I felt for him. I knew that what hurt most in the general rejoicing was the assumption that Paul's life had been a useless irrelevance, a disaster best forgotten.

To me it did not seem like that. Yes, I was glad he was dead. But at the same time, I owed him an incalculable debt. If our value as human beings lies in what we do for each other, Paul had done a very great deal: he had, at the very least, opened the eyes of his mother to the suffering that was in the world, and had brought her to understand something of the redemptive force it was capable of generating. I had been broken, but I had been put together again, and I had met many who bore far more inspiring witness than I to the strength inherent in the mending process. What Paul had done for me was to challenge me to face up to the reality of my own situation; and he had handed me a key to unlock reserves buried so deep I hadn't suspected their existence.

Self-knowledge comes to us only in the dark times, when we are stripped of illusion and naked to truth. If Paul had helped me towards even a little understanding, how could I agree that he had lived to no purpose? He had taught me a lesson, quite unwittingly, and now that he was no longer there, I owed it to him not to forget.

(Blessings, M. Craig, pp. 115–16)

The grit and the pearl

205 Childhood is the beginning of life and in the natural order of things, should be as far away as possible from death. Yet the cradle and the grave can be fearfully close: either a child dies or another can experience death through the loss of a close relation or friend. At the same time most of us have limited contact with suffering and the capacity it can produce to undergo an exceptional degree of endurance. Suffering is a fact of life. We can fight it or be overwhelmed by it. Sometimes we have to stay with it, which is where endurance comes in, but no-one need do this alone. Around the pain something can happen and the whole experience can be redeemed by love.

We cannot deny the fact of pain and our very humanity cries out for the elimination of suffering in children. But we can learn patience and endure the suffering with them. Take an oyster for example. It reminds us that pain can be transformed into something of great value. The little piece of grit, so irritating and distressing, is slowly covered and changed into a pearl. In the same way, a piece of grit in the human tissue may cause an abscess and it remains true that for some, the hurt of handicap continues as a throbbing and resented pain. We do not know the oyster's secret but believe that for us it is the love of God which when allowed, lubricates the hurting places in our spirits and changes them so wonderfully. This is not to say God designs handicapped children but when one comes he bestows special grace to help in times of need. We have to accept after all that God is the creator of a world in which these sorts of things happen.

(*Signs of the Kingdom*, the address for Lent 3: 'Endurance' by J. Goodall)

Wanted – just as he was

206 Christopher Nolan is 21. He nearly died at birth from asphyxiation. But he survived, with severe brain damage. He cannot speak; he cannot hear well; and he cannot move himself. After an enormous struggle he learned to type, with a stick attached to his head, and this year his book *Under the Eye of the Clock* won the prize for the Whitbread Book of the year.

***Under the Eye of the Clock* is really the incredible story of Christopher Nolan's childhood, although he disguises himself and tells his story as if it were fiction . . .**

'Looking through his tears he saw her as she bent low in order to look into his eyes. "I never prayed for you to be born crippled," she said, "I wanted you to be full of life, able to run and jump and talk like Yvonne. But you are you, you are Joseph not Yvonne. Listen here Joseph, you can see, you can hear, you can think, you can understand everything you hear, you like your food, you like nice clothes, you are loved by me and Dad. We love you just as you are." Pussing still, snivelling still, he was listening to his mother's voice. She spoke sort of matter-of-factly but he blubbered moaning sounds. His mother had her say and that was that. She got on with her work while he got on with his crying.

'The decision arrived at that day was burnt forever in his mind. He was only three years in age but he was now fanning the only spark he saw, his being alive and more immediate, his being wanted just as he was.'

When Christopher Nolan received his prize for that book his mother gave the acceptance speech which he had written, and he used it to speak about the handicapped and about abortion.

'Tonight a crippled man is taking his place on the world literary stage. Tonight is my night for laughing, for crying tears of joy. But wait, my brothers hobble after me hinting, "What about silent us? Can we too have a voice?" Tonight I am speaking for them.

'Tonight is the happiest night of my life. Imagine what I would have missed if the doctors had not revived me on that September day long ago.'

(A Disabled Person? By S. Brown in *My World*, ed. S. Brown pp. 39–41, quoting C. Nolan)

'The presence of God in the heart of the dark'

207 In the teeth of the evidence, I do not believe that any suffering is ultimately absurd or pointless. But it is often difficult to go on convincing oneself. When someone we love dies or meets with a violent accident, when a child is brutally murdered or dies of cancer, when a deep relationship is broken up, or when any disappointment or upheaval strikes, despair may set in. We are marooned in misery. Shaking our fists, pounding the air, we ask that despairing and futile question, why. Why, why, why? Most of all, why ME? What have I done to deserve it? If I were God, I wouldn't allow such awful things to happen. How can there be a God of love when the world is full of suffering? . . .

It's not really surprising, in a world which spawned Auschwitz, Hiroshima and Vietnam, and which seems now hell-bent on self-destruction, that so many have turned away from the mere idea of God, and from the possibility that life has a meaning and an underlying purpose . . .

Yet, isn't it at least possible that in the course of time all things do work together for good? In the concentration camp of Ravensbrück, that graveyard of so many human hopes and desires, an unknown prisoner wrote this prayer on a torn scrap of wrapping-paper, and left it by the body of a dead child:

> O lord, remember not only the men and women of good will, but also those of ill-will. But do not remember all the suffering they have inflicted on us; remember the fruits we have bought, thanks to this suffering – our comradeship, our loyalty, our humility, our courage, our generosity, the greatness of heart which has grown out of all this, and when they come to judgement, let all the fruits which we have borne be their forgiveness.

That prayer, with its white-hot humanity, seems to me to proclaim and affirm the presence of God in the heart of the dark. And if we dislike or are embarrassed by the word 'God', as so many are, we can substitute another word or phrase – Love, perhaps.

(Blessings, M. Craig, pp. 135–36)

208   He is the nameless presence alongside all those who are suddenly cast down into the darkness of loneliness and foreboding as disaster strikes in everyday life: the person suddenly bereaved of that which made his life tolerable, indeed meaningful, and especially the one suddenly afflicted by incapacitating illness. After the initial shock has been faced and absorbed, the spark of hope flickers inwardly. It leads us to a faith which enables us to act according to the instructions of a source beyond our own cognition. He is that spark within that ignites the hope; he is the faith that leads us on the uncharted path through darkness to ultimate light, a light far more radiant than the light of reason at its most brilliant . . .

Christ is the master of our darkness.

(Gethsemane, M. Israel, p. 100)

DEATH

209 Death treads the corridors of power, and the lowest peasant's hut,
And is indifferent to both.
Death frees the captive, fills the hungry, releases the suffering,
But haunts the rich.
Death has won every war since time began, without firing a shot.
Death drives men crazy with fear
But is their friend, when all other friends fail.
Death is a gateway or a brick wall
Depending on your view.
Death is kind to individuals but also
Breaks hearts and splits families.
Death is an alpha and omega and yet
Never both.
Death is the most common biological complaint
100% of all people will catch it.
But is it a complaint?
Death is a well known fact,
About which nothing is known.
Death is universally disliked,
While it saves men from the infinitely worse process of dying.
Death is?
Death is.

(*It's Important to Me*, poem 'Death' by A. Bullock)

210 Death is a fact of life. If we know nothing else about life, we know that we shall die at some time. All living things have a cycle of birth, growth and death. Death is a natural process. But it is unknown what lies beyond it; and it is natural for us as humans to fear the unknown.

From ancient times people have tried to account for what may happen to us after death. We know that our bodies will decay and that the atoms which came together to create us will disperse once more into the universe.

But what of the 'essence' of us: our thoughts, our feelings, our memories: our 'souls'?

Most religions believe that all is not lost at death and that the core of our being – what makes us distinct from anyone else who ever lived – returns to whence it came i.e. a Supreme Creator/God. And there is a strong yearning in us to believe that all the energy and essence of all which we know exists is not dissipated at death.

What do *you* think about life and death? is it all the result of chance factors? Or is there more to it all than what we see and know?

(L. Stephenson)

Facing up to death

211 For most people, the question of life after death is not so much settled as ignored. To face it and think it through would involve raising too many disturbing questions, so it is simply not faced. But it will not do to leave it like that. To ignore this question is the attitude of the moral coward. It is important: surely everyone would agree. Whether death destroys personality, or is a step onwards to a new life in a new environment, is a momentous question, which every single person ought to face, consider, and in due course answer.

It is possible to come to terms with death from a thoroughly mature, considered humanistic position; and it is manifestly possible to do so from a mature, considered Christian position. But it is difficult, if not impossible, to do so if our attitude is to refuse to consider the question at all. That way we condemn ourselves to a life-time of self-deception and corroding inner fear, unable to accept either mortality or immortality, either a noble humanism that faces death as the final extinction of a life well lived, or a true Christianity which looks on and beyond to a life with God.

(*Hereafter*, D. Winter, pp. 15–16)

212 The event of physical death is an awesome moment. There is no absolute proof of survival of any aspect of the personality. While the data of psychical research are not negligible, and indeed spiritualists are convinced that they can enjoy meaningful communication with the deceased, there is a veil between the living and those who have passed beyond mortal life which has not yet been successfully penetrated by objective means. This to me is exactly as it should be. Until we have reached the spiritual stature of Christ, the full meaning of resurrection and immortality will be hidden from us. The awe of death and the uncertainty of personal survival are the foundation on which the corner-stones of faith are laid.

What is it that survives the immediate death of the physical body? Of course, to the atheistic humanist this question is pitiful, for since to him matter alone is real, there can be no survival of anything resembling a conscious personality once the brain has disintegrated. But to those of us who have cultivated an inner life of meditation and prayer while here on earth, and have lived in self-giving relationship (relationship in depth, as the phrase goes) with others, especially our loved ones, the introspective fact of an inner identity, or soul, becomes ever clearer.

(*Summons to Life*, M. Israel, pp. 139, 141)

213 Human life does come to an end, and however painful the realisation of this may be, we do psychological harm to ourselves by taking refuge behind talk of sleep or release or passing on. There is a tragic finality about death which we must take seriously, or it is not death we are talking about. The Christian may wish to add further comments of his own, but unless what he has to say is based on the reality of death, he is building on a lie. . . .
For resurrection, whatever it means, is not a resumption of life after a brief interruption. It is a new creation, *ex nihilo*, out of the nothingness of death. . . . death remains an impenetrable darkness. But the darkness is filled with the creative presence of God.

(*Death and After*, H. Richards, pp. 25, 30)

214 We all suffer from this fatal disease of life, and yet society does everything in its power to make us forget that sooner or later we come to an end.

We're none of us ready for death, we thrust it out of our consciousness; one of the most tragic things about so many funerals is not just the sense of shock at the terrible intruder, reminding everyone of their own mortality, but also the sense of lost time, of missed opportunities. We live as if we were immortal, but time is not on our side; by the time the funeral comes, it's too late to say, 'If only . . .'

But the real problem of death concerns not sadness or a sense of loss, not even our own mortality: it is to do with the question that mortality asks us – what, after all, is this whole rigmarole about? Are we born just to die, and does that inevitable death make all our achievements, our dreams, hopes, loves and longings of as much worth as an empty cigarette packet? At the end of the game, says the Spanish proverb, king and pawn go back into the same box.

(*God for Nothing*, R. MacKenna, pp. 22–3)

215 There are some thoughts that come upon us frequently but which we push away as too morbid, too depressing. Such a thought is death. There are reminders of death all around. The long column in the evening paper, death on the roads, flood, fire, accident, the news bulletin. We get used to the fact of death. But we insulate ourselves against its reality. We seldom think: I must die.

Yet death is an ingredient of life, the finale, the end-product. It is more sensible to live with the thought of death than to try and shoo it away, frightened by it. A person who lives in full consciousness of the fact that he must die is not morbid. He is . . . realistic. For death is real, as real as life. And the thought of death makes life vivid, active and wholesome. It teaches proportion, stops a man or woman getting too attached to things that are not lasting and indispensable. A man who rents a house for a short time will not spend a fortune on it. He will see what is important, put it right, and leave the trimmings. And life, for any man, for any woman, is a short-term lease.

(*Last Thing at Night*, H. Lavery, p. 65)

Live for today

216 Eleven months have passed since the cancer in my body was first detected – eleven months of the limited life I am expected to have left, the original sentence being about one year. The medical prognosis is still the same, and the latest scan showed a further increase in the tumour. The future officially is bleak, and I am getting used to people looking at me as a dying man under sentence of death. Nothing is certain. I'm not out of the wood yet. Everything is a matter of faith.

That is why I have written the book at this stage. I am not looking back at a painful episode in the past; the difficulties are still with me. I am not writing from a position of comparative safety; I am at present in the thick of it, with humanly speaking no answers, no certainties, no proof of healing – nothing except a somewhat daunting unknown. And yet in reality, my position is not fundamentally different from that of anyone else. No one knows what the future holds. Our lives are full of ifs and buts and supposings. Nothing is sure apart from death. Whether we like it or not, everyone has to live by faith. The *object* of faith is naturally of absolute importance, and may vary considerably. Some will trust in God, others in money, luck, prosperity, health, medicine, philosophy or wishful thinking. But no one can escape the risk of faith when it comes to the greatest issues of life and death. . . .

'What if you are not healed?' I am sometimes asked. Although it does not help to dwell on that question too much, I realise that it is a perfectly fair one; and that is where the Christian hope for the future is so enormously important. Of course I cannot *know* that I shall have ten to twenty years more to live. I cannot *know* that I have even one. But that is also true of every one of us. With all our planning for the future, we need to live a day at a time and enjoy each day as a gift from God. 'This is the day which the Lord has made; let us rejoice and be glad in it' (Psalm 118:24). Some Christians speak of the *sacrament of the present moment*: we need to live, not just a day at a time, but moment by moment, seeking to do God's will for each moment of our life. That alone is the way in which we can know the fullness of God's joy and peace.

(*Fear No Evil*, D. Watson, pp. 152, 157)

Our attitude to death affects our attitude to life

217 Many people today, if asked their attitude towards the question of life after death, would reply: 'Does it really matter? Haven't we quite enough to do in this world without bothering about another? If there is another life after death, we shall know all about it when the time comes. In the meantime let's make the best we can of the present one.'

This is an understandable attitude, and in a measure commendable. If our concern with the next world is so absorbing that it distracts us from fulfilling our tasks and obligations in this one, it is clearly open to the charge . . . of a selfish otherworldliness.

But it is possible to fall into the opposite error and to suppose that faith in a future life has no practical bearing upon how we live in this one. . . . Belief in life beyond death brings with it a vast expansion of our mental and spiritual horizon, so that we see our life in an entirely new perspective. No longer do we look on it as an existence limited in duration, and liable to be cut short at any moment by illness or accident, even maybe before it has reached its prime. We see our life on earth as little more than a training or apprenticeship for what lies ahead, though a training which has immensely important bearing on the future. We believe, indeed, that in God's purpose there is a work for us to do here . . . We need not, therefore, feel unduly disappointed or frustrated if, through illness or some other cause, cherished projects have to be laid aside or we are cut off at the height of our powers. We have all eternity before us.

It is not difficult to see how this realisation of unlimited extent of time and opportunity can give to our lives and character a quiet serenity and assurance which can radiate to others something of the peace of God. The life surrendered to the God of eternity is not spent in a vain rush to overtake the fleeting moments.

(*The Gate of Life*, J. Winslow, pp. 86–7)

218 Very often as we live, so we die. Death is nothing but a continuation of life, the completion of life ... This life is not the end; people who believe it is, fear death. If it was properly explained that death was nothing but going home to God, then there would be no fear.

(Mother Teresa in *Meditations on The Way of the Cross*, Mother Teresa and Brother Roger, p. 54)

An out-of-the-body experience

219 'You won't know a thing', the nurses told me as they wheeled me down to the theatre. 'You'll just fall asleep, and next minute you'll wake up back in your bed in the ward.'

I never told them how wrong they were.

For a start, it was more than just 'falling asleep'. When I succumbed to the anaesthetist's pin-prick I was transported to a world so different from the one I'd left that there wasn't even the faintest memory to remind me of it.

Yet this new world wasn't new in the sense of being unfamiliar. Quite the contrary, I was filled with a sense of being fully 'at home' in this space-world of yellow sunlight filled with floating golddust. This was so much my home, I would swear I had never once left it, never once ever briefly visited any other existence. I had been here forever, would remain here forever and would not want it otherwise. My contentment was not passive however, but spiced with hope and excitement as I contemplated drawing nearer to the distant source of the sunlight that surrounded me. Somewhere just ahead (I'd be there soon) the light was magnetically intense, flashing and bouncing off the thickening golddust, and I longed to be drawn into it.

Suddenly, I was startled by noises from another place. A note of alarm jarred my golden peace and I looked about to see the cause. Something was happening below me.

'There! How's that? Any sign?'

'No, nothing! Still nothing!'

'Oh my God! Come on. Come on!'

Above this exchange, I was no more than some kind of floating emotion. I now changed from irritation at the intrusion into my contentment to curiosity as I watched the scene below. Slowly, it seemed, the panic rose to touch me and I realized what was going on. The surgeon and the anaesthetist wanted me to breathe.

I knew at once what that would mean. If I breathed for them, I should have to leave the sun, the gold, the peace and the hope that was more of a 'home' than I'd ever known. Worse, it would mean I should have to rejoin some awful forgotten place where I had been distressed.

No. Not that. Where's the gold? Where's the light?

A voice shouted quietly, the whispered shout of ultimate desperation.

'Oh please, *please*! For God's sake, come on!'

Confusion gave way to compassion. I'd have to breathe for them. How could I refuse?

Very deliberately, knowing fully what I was doing, and what it was costing, I took a deep breath.

I drew it somewhere near the ceiling.

I expelled it from the table.

The shouts of relief hit my ears in stereo.

'That's it! She's there!'

'Thank God! For a minute I thought . . .'

I disappeared into blackness and woke in the recovery ward.

After being moved to a quiet convalescent hospital I had plenty of time to ponder on my experience. Perhaps such 'dreams' were common. But other patients had spoken only of going to sleep and waking back in bed. I hesitated to share my own story for fear of ridicule or, from the staff, professional reassurance intended to refute all thought of theatre crises.

But I believed then, and still do, that I had indeed hovered between this life and the next, and that I had been allowed to return to my family. I know that if I'd been drawn into that light-source I'd never have been tempted away from it. I wouldn't have heard the panic, or even known I'd ever lived anywhere else but in that sublime light.

So I asked myself, as I sat outside in the autumn sun and watched the apples drop quietly from the trees in the hospital orchard: 'Why am I here and not there?'

(*Not Quite Heaven*, B. Courtie, pp. 39–41)

A plea for more openness about death and bereavement

220 Someone who is dying brings us up against our own fear: a fear that we all know; that one day we are going to die ourselves. Most of us don't want to think about that; so we retreat and look away. Not always, but often. And that can isolate the dying person terribly. Other people won't talk about it and they pretend it isn't happening . . .

It would be good if society could be more open about death. If we could start to take our children to funerals, for example. If you take your child to the funeral of somebody who isn't very important – a great aunt whom they have never met, perhaps – then a funeral and death becomes a normal and acceptable part of things. And we shouldn't hide our grief and our distress if somebody is very ill. When my own mother was dying of cancer and had an operation my children were only little, and they were very upset. I said to them that Gran was very ill; and the doctors couldn't make her better but they could make her comfortable. We talked about it, and we could be open. If I had hidden my fear and my distress it would have created more fear and distress in them, and it would have become a vicious circle. . . . What I want to say about dying is that it's all right to hurt – both as a widow and as somebody who is dying. It is very painful to be a widow. It is agonizing and terrible. And it is agonizing and terrible to know that you are going to lose your life. But hurting is all right. You are not going to fall apart at the seams. You can hurt and you can survive. It is important not to run away from hurt. It's awful; but it doesn't go on for ever. If you let it flow around you, and go wherever it takes you, then it's all right.

('We die with the dying' by P. Yorkstone in *My World*, ed. S. Brown, pp. 45–7)

Separation from loved ones

221 There can be few of us who have not at some period of our lives suffered the pain of bereavement through the death of some dearly-loved relation or friend. There is a blank space left in our lives almost as though a part of ourselves had been torn away. And if we believe that death is the end for all of us, there will be left only the rather sad, if cherished, memory of a friendship which can never be recaptured. If, on the other hand, we believe that death is the gateway to fuller life, and that therefore our departed friends and loved ones are more alive than ever, our whole outlook is different. There will indeed be a measure of sadness because the beloved presence has been taken from us. There is a gap at the table and by the fireside. The stimulus of our talks together, the sharing of common interests, the holidays enjoyed together on the hills or by the sea, the games we played and the jokes we shared; all these are over, and we cannot help missing them. But somehow there is a difference. The memory of these things is a happy one. We recall them with delight. We believe that those who have passed on share them with us. At times we may even be conscious of their nearness to us.

(*The Gate of Life*, J. Winslow, p. 91)

222 Death is nothing at all . . . 'I have only slipped away into the next room, I am I, and you are you. Whatever we were to each other, that we are still. Call me by my old familiar name, speak to me in the same easy way you always used. Put no difference in your tone; wear no forced air of solemnity or sorrow, laugh as we always laughed together.

'Play, smile, think of me, pray for me. Let my name be ever the household word that it always was. Let it be spoken without effort, without the ghost of a shadow upon it. Life means all that it ever meant. It is the same as it ever was. There is absolutely unbroken continuity. Why should I be out of mind because I am out of sight? I am waiting for you for an interval, somewhere very near, just around the corner . . . All is well'.

(D. Sweetman in *The Trident*, quoting Canon Henry Scott Holland, a Victorian priest.

223 There is the constantly recurring question whether we shall know and meet and recognise each other again on the other side of death. One thing is quite certain – Christian orthodoxy does not teach the immortality of the soul; it teaches the resurrection of the body. We do not mean by that the resurrection of this body as it is. For many of us the last thing in the world that we would want is the resurrection of the burden and the weariness of this mortal body. We would never wish for the resurrection of the actual body with which a man was smashed up in an accident or died with an incurable disease. It so happens that Greek has no word for personality, and the resurrection of the body means the survival of the personality; it means that in the life beyond, you will still be you, and I will still be I. This is in opposition, for instance, to the beliefs of Stoicism. The Stoics believed that God is a fire, more pure than any earthly fire; and what gives man life is that a spark, a *scintilla*, of the divine fire comes and lives in his body. When he dies the spark of divine fire, goes back to its source and is reabsorbed in the life of all things, in the being of God. That is the immortality of the soul, but it is not the survival of personality. . . .

This means that in the beyond we will meet each other again. But I have never been able to see in this only the joy of meeting again those whom we have loved and lost awhile. We shall have to meet again those whom we have wronged; those to whom we have been disloyal; those whom we have hurt; those whom we have deceived. There will be no doubt the reuniting of love, but there will also be confrontation with truth . . .

The meetings again will have their joy, but they will also have their shame, but we can hope and believe that in the heavenly places those who have been forgiven will also learn to forgive.

(*Testament of Faith*, W. Barclay, pp. 62–4)

Approaching death

224 We live in a day when men try to deny or ignore their mortal natures. In a death-denying culture we emphasize the values of youth, beauty, health, and vigor, as if there were something disloyal or inhuman about that accumulation of years that moves a man towards his death. Just because we tend to deny the physical reality of death, we are in a poor position to build a philosophy of life that is adequate for both life and death. The effort to escape the full meaning of the reality of physical death means that we are inclined to ignore also the responsibilities that are commensurate with our mortal natures. If we live only for the enjoyment of each today, and avoid its responsibilities, we may well fail to accept the important spiritual disciplines that best prepare us for today, tomorrow, and eternity.

(*Understanding Prayer*, E. Jackson, p. 198)

225 Victor Hugo could write: 'I feel immortality in myself. The earth gives me its generous sap but heaven lights me with the reflection of unknown worlds. You say the soul is nothing but the resultant of bodily powers. Why, then, is my soul more luminous as the bodily powers begin to fail? Winter is on my head, but eternal spring is in my heart. The nearer I approach the end, the plainer I hear round me the immortal symphonies of the world to come ... For half a century I have been writing my thoughts in prose and verse; but I feel I have not said one thousandth part of what is in me! When I have gone down to the grave I shall have ended my day's work; but another day will begin next morning. Life closes in twilight, but opens with the dawn.'

(*The Gate of Life*, J. Winslow, pp. 32-3)

226 As I do not believe that earthly life can bring any lasting satisfaction, the prospect of death holds no terrors. Those saints who pronounced themselves in love with death displayed, I consider, the best of sense: not a Freudian death-wish. Likewise Pastor Bonhoeffer when he told his Nazi guards, as they took him away to be executed, that for them it was an end but for him a beginning; in that place of darkest evil he, the victim, shining and radiant. The world that I shall soon be leaving seems more than ever beautiful; especially its remoter parts, grass and trees and sea and rivers and little streams and sloping hills, where the image of eternity is more clearly stamped than among streets and houses. Those I love I can love even more, since I have nothing to ask of them but their love; the passion to accumulate possessions, or to be noticed and important, is too evidently absurd to be any longer entertained.

A sense of how extraordinarily happy I have been, and of enormous gratitude to my creator, overwhelms me often. I believe with a passionate, unshakeable conviction that in all circumstances and at all times life is a blessed gift; that the spirit which animates it is one of love, not hate or indifference, of light, not darkness, of creativity, not destruction, of order, not chaos; that, since all life, men, creatures, plants, as well as insensate matter, and all that is known about it, now and henceforth, has been benevolently, not malevolently, conceived, when the eyes see no more and the mind thinks no more, and this hand now writing is inert, whatever lies beyond will similarly be benevolently, not malevolently conceived. If it is nothing, then for nothingness I offer thanks; if another mode of existence, with this old worn-out husk of a body left behind, like a butterfly extricating itself from its chrysalis, and this floundering, muddled mind, now at best seeing through a glass darkly, given a longer range and a new precision, then for that likewise I offer thanks.

(M. Muggeridge in *What I Believe*, ed. M. Booth, p. 68)

Belief in life after death

227 What does it mean to pray for the dead? Are we asking the Lord to act unjustly? Certainly not. By our prayer, we bear witness that the dead have not lived in vain. We show that as well as the many worthless things they did in their lives, they also sowed the seed of charity. We pray for them with love and gratitude, we remember their presence among us. And our prayer for them must be supported by our lives. If we do not bear fruit in our lives of what the dead have taught us, our prayer for them will be feeble indeed. We must be able to say, 'Look Lord, this man lived and made me love him, he gave me examples to follow and I follow them'. The day will come when we shall be able to say, 'The good that you see in my life is not mine; he gave me it, take it and let it be for his glory, perhaps for his forgiveness'. . . .

The life of each one of us does not end at death on this earth and birth into heaven. . . . In the dead we no longer belong completely to this world, in us the dead still belong to history. Prayer for the dead is vital, it expresses the totality of our common life.

(A. Bloom in *Courage to Pray*, A. Bloom and G. LeFevre, pp. 59–60)

228 In the God whom Jesus came to reveal there are two qualities which make a life to come a necessity in the divine scheme of things. There is *the justice of God*. No one can say that in this world virtue gains its reward and wickedness its punishment. If there is to be any justice in life, a new world must be called in to redress the balance of the old. There is *the love of God*. In this world young lives are cut off too soon, and often in a way that just does not make sense. If there is no place in which these lives receive their chances to flourish, to blossom in their beauty, to realise their potential, to be what this life never allowed them to be, then it is not love which is at the centre of this world.

(*Testament of Faith*, W. Barclay, p. 56)

229 I am run over by a train and my body is cut in two.
But what is it that has been cut?
My body or my life?
A chemical combination or my light?
An agglomeration of cells or my love.
No, no-one can cut my life which is eternal.
No-one can cut my light which continues to exist.
No-one can cut my love.
We are eternal, we cannot die because we are grafted to the eternal life which is God.
We are grafted to the light which is Christ.
We are united to the love which is the Holy Spirit.
And no-one can cut the Holy Spirit in two.
No-one can take away from us our participation in the divine life.

(*The Desert in the City*, C. Carretto, p. 71)

230 Oh, God, death is so still, so utterly still.
   Death is more still than the quietest meadow on a summer day. Stiller than the whitest snows of a winter hillside. More deeply still than the deepest stillness of a starry night.
   There is such peace in death, for the spirit is lost in the bliss of some absolute dream.
   Death is perfect acceptance, perfect understanding.
   Death is the perfect knowing.
   'Be still and know that I am God,' you said. The living can never attain that absolute perfection of stillness and knowing. Only the dead.
   But so profound is their stillness this we do know: In you they live.

(*I've got to Talk to Somebody, God*, M. Holmes, pp. 117–18)

231 We pray for all those whom we love who have died. We give thanks for their lives and for the privilege of knowing them.
And we ask that GOD, in his mercy, will take them to himself and bring them to fulfilment in him.   *Amen*

(J. Thompson)

INDEX OF AUTHORS

Abhishiktananda 163, 168
Askew, Eddie 30, 88, 138, 194
Barclay, William 1, 96, 114, 169, 191, 223, 228
Bishop, Paula 7
Bloom, Anthony 2, 68, 150, 151, 158, 166, 227
Bonhoeffer, Dietrich 3
Booth, Mark 18, 55, 226
Brent, Barbara 46
Brother Roger 64, 173
Brown, Shelagh 97, 131, 133, 202, 206, 220
Bullock, A. 209
Carretto, Carlo 73, 165, 229
Challen, Peter 97
Conway, John 75
Corbishley, Thomas 194
Courtie, Brenda 219
Craig, Mary 67, 196, 198, 199, 204, 207
Dunlop, Ian 106
Edwards, David 89, 90, 95, 121, 135, 147
Einstein, Albert 55
Ellwood, W. 60
Foster, Richard 157
Fromm, Erich 42
Furlong, Monica 59, 156, 159, 177
Gallagher, Rosemary 110, 146, 203
Gallico, Paul 160
Garvey, Jon 49
Gibbard, Mark 83, 86, 93
Goldman, Ronald 53
Goodall, Janet 205
Grollenberg, Lucas 137
Gullick, Etta 6, 63, 152
Hare Duke, Michael 50, 51
Harries, Richard 62, 65, 78, 167, 174, 175, 188, 189
Henesy, Michael 110, 146, 203
Hollings, Michael 6, 63, 152
Holmes, Marjorie 17, 43, 141, 148, 161, 197, 230
Israel, Martin 13, 16, 26, 41, 45, 70, 176, 208, 212
Jackson, Edgar 4, 9, 12, 24, 32, 149, 155, 224
Jasper, Tony 143
Johnson, M. 82
Jung, Carl 105

King, Martin Luther   38, 58, 66, 84, 124, 178, 179
Kossoff, David   20, 142
Laski, Marghanita   151
Lavery, Hugh   19, 28, 92, 108, 215
Lealman, Brenda   47, 48
LeFevre, Georges   150
Loukes, Harold   136
MacKenna, Richard   14, 29, 34, 39, 52, 54, 85, 119, 200, 214
Mayne, Michael   112, 113, 116, 130, 192, 201
Meegan, Micheal   15, 21, 23, 27, 35, 37, 71, 87, 123, 139, 171, 172, 184
Morley, Janet   186
Mother Teresa   120, 129, 218
Muggeridge, Malcolm   226
Neary, Donal   134
Nouwen, Henri   11, 36, 79, 103, 115, 140
Packer, J. I.   33
Polkinghorne, J.   56
Powell, John   5, 170
Rae, D.   128
Rees, Lynne   61
Rees, T.   101
Rhymes, Douglas   117, 118, 162
Richard, Cliff   81
Richards, H. J.   99, 100, 213
Robinson, Edward   47, 48
Schutz, S. P.   143
Sheen, Martin   18
Smith-Cameron, Ivor   69
Southall, J.   80
Stephenson, Louise   8, 210
Sweetman, D.   154
Taylor, John   68, 94, 98, 107, 144
Thompson, Jan   22, 40, 102, 109, 111, 125, 180, 231
Thompson, Jim   77
Temple, D.   132
Topping, Frank   74, 76, 122, 164
Trueblood, E.   10
Vanier, Jean   72, 126, 127, 181, 182, 195
Ward, Keith   153
Watson, David   31, 57, 91, 190, 193, 216
Weldon, Fay   25
West, Morris   44
Winslow, Jack   217, 221, 225
Winter, David   211
Wood, W.   133
Yorkstone, Paddy   220